Handcrafted
COUNTRY

COUNTRY LIVING

Handcrafted
COUNTRY

Decorative Projects for a Beautiful Home

TEXT BY

Mary Seehafer Sears and Eleanor Levie

HEARST BOOKS

A Division of Sterling Publishing Co., Inc.

New York

This book was previously published under the title
Country Living Handmade Country: Old-Fashioned Crafts and Timeless Keepsakes.

PRODUCED BY SMALLWOOD & STEWART, INC., NEW YORK CITY
EDITOR: LINDA HETZER
ART DIRECTOR: SUSI OBERHELMAN
DESIGNER: AMANDA WILSON
ILLUSTRATOR: EDWARD LAM

Library of Congress Cataloging-in-Publication Data
Available upon request.

10 9 8 7 6 5 4 3 2

First paperback edition 2003
Published by Hearst Books
A Division of Sterling Publishing Co., Inc.
387 Park Avenue South, New York, NY 10016

www.countryliving.com

Distributed in Canada by Sterling Publishing
c/o Canadian Manda Group, One Atlantic Avenue, Suite 105
Toronto, Ontario, Canada M6K 3E7
Distributed in Australia by Capricorn Link (Australia) Pty. Ltd.
P.O. Box 704, Windsor, NSW 2756 Australia

Printed in China

ISBN 1-58816-249-4

CONTENTS

Foreword

Of all the subjects we explore at *Country Living*, the one most near and dear to my heart is that of crafts. Whether it is a painted floor, a papered bandbox, or a dried floral wreath, chances are it is a project I have tackled. My parents, who nurtured all signs of my creativity, supplied paints and crayons the minute my hands could hold them. I was a demon with knitting needles before grammar school and got the arts-and-crafts medal at summer camp for my pinch pots.

As a young working girl in New York, I careened through a series of jobs until one day I stumbled onto one on a fledgling crafts magazine, where I was given the title of managing editor. But, since there were only three of us, I also helped execute many of the projects for photography.

By the time I was given my own crafts magazine, *American Home Crafts*, several years later, I had a house full of needlepoint pillows, crocheted afghans, and painted boxes—not to mention the ubiquitous macramé plant hangers. This was in the early seventies. Magazines were just beginning to show crafts projects for the home and Americans were discovering the joys of working with their hands for fun and

fulfillment rather than necessity. Finally, with the celebration of the Bicentennial came a revival of American Period design and its attendant crafts. Do-it-yourself projects were elevated to an art, and crafts and crafting for the home became the major way we personalized our environments.

Through the years, we have celebrated the handmade at *Country Living* and are delighted to share some of our favorite projects; we hope they will inspire and encourage you.

RACHEL NEWMAN
Editor Emerita, *Country Living*

Introduction

 *andmade Country* is a book about decorating with and living among old, sentimental things that add warmth and charm to a house. Well-loved objects with the patina of time are especially cherished nowadays, when so many items are made by machine. Rescue an old rocking chair from the dump and bring an heirloom back to life. Stitch a quilt or a sampler, paint a tabletop, stencil a stairway, and your handiwork will be appreciated for years to come.

This book shows how to celebrate the homemade and handcrafted, how to glorify the past by creating a rustic twig planter, refinishing a picture frame, or reusing a vintage grain bin as a side table. Cherished pieces enrich a home bit by bit, and many are cloaked with memories. The country look has evolved over the years, but the personal always prevails. A welcoming home is inhabited with the homespun, not the mass-made. This sort of decorating appeals, whether a room is filled to the rafters or carefully edited to be spare and serene.

Handmade Country contains five chapters filled with photographs and step-by-step instructions for making things. The first chapter, "A Nod to Nature," encourages hunting and gathering instincts. Vines, shells, flowers, and twigs are natural grace notes for the home. The paper chapter will have you pulling out scissors and glue to relive your days as a child artist, this time with grown-up results. Silhouettes, decoupage, and collage are all within your grasp. Paint is the subject of the third chapter. Making a checkerboard floorcloth and leaf-printed curtains may be just the start of your adventures with a paintbrush. Hooked rugs, old-fashioned penny rugs, and appliquéd table runners have warmed the hearts and souls of men and women for centuries. Find out how to make them, and more, in our fourth chapter on fabric. The final chapter, "A Link With the Past," encourages you to play lost-and-found with discarded treasures. Even if you can't do "craft" things, using something old in a new way is an exercise open to all. Take tables, for instance. We show creative coffee tables, a sawhorse table relocated from barn to foyer, even a cemetery gate used as a table base. Study every page and discover more ideas for reusing the old in new ways.

Do you have a piece of pretty wallpaper you might frame? An old dresser in the garage that cries out for color? A game board in the attic that's not being used? Warm up rooms with a single doll on a windowsill, or a heap of dried sunflowers on the mantel. Enrich your life with the handmade, the lovingly stitched, the natural. Find your inspiration here.

a nod to
NATURE

Each time a fall leaf is pressed between sheets of waxed paper, another nature craft begins. Preserving and displaying things from the earth is a tradition that never grows old. Shell pictures, potpourri, dried apples on a string—nature's bounty has always inspired creativity, and offers a window on the changing seasons. Fresh flowers and sweet-smelling herbs are the basis of spring and summer crafts; leaf and pumpkin projects signal autumn's harvest; pomanders and evergreen swags herald the winter holidays

For maximum impact and a rich visual effect, display layer upon layer of nature-walk treasures in a single place. In the foyer of an early-eighteenth-century stone house (opposite), reed baskets, seashells, fallen birds' nests, dried flowers, and pinecones mingle on an old farm table. Sunflowers (right) keep their straight stems when hung upside down to dry.

and warm the house during the long stretch to spring. Then the pussy willows open, bulbs sprout, fresh greens appear, and the crafting begins anew.

Artists of long ago had to rely on materials from their own backyards. They used what was abundant and at hand. After a day of work a pioneer farmer whittled a piece of wood by the fire and displayed the finished carving on his mantelpiece while his wife made a cornhusk doll to amuse a young child.

Today, we gather and create in much the same way, but our bounty is easier to find. Craft stores, florists, garden centers, and catalogues supply any material, no matter how unusual. A seashell project can be assembled miles from a shoreline, and pinecone wreaths turned out from a workshop in the desert. Success is a given: It's hard to make mistakes with natural materials. And enthusiasm can

Make potpourri with ingredients gathered from countryside and garden: herbs and dried flowers, fir cones, citrus peel, cinnamon sticks, nuts, leaves, and bark. Add orrisroot (a fixative) and a generous blend of ground spices, such as allspice, nutmeg, cloves, and cinnamon. For a stronger fragrance add essential oils of cedarwood, cinnamon, clove, orange, or frankincense. For more color, add dried flower heads. Let the potpourri sit in a covered container for two to three weeks to allow the fragrance to develop.

snowball. The heavy book used to press flowers is soon abandoned for a flower press. An unused guest room is recast as a studio. One grapevine wreath, successfully executed, results in a row of wreaths to give as gifts.

The things you can make from nature's bounty are as diverse as nature itself. Many projects start with flowers and herbs, simply because they're so beautiful and easy to find. Fresh bouquets make delightful decorations all year round and are always a welcome gift. Set an arrangement in a simple container that suits the mood of the cuttings. Made from flowers gathered in early morning as the dew lifts, pressed-flower bookmarks are charming.

Wreaths represent the circle of life and, as a symbol of eternity, are often associated with holidays and weddings. Boxwood, grapevine, and evergreen wreaths are classic decorating tools that never grow old, and they're easy to make from the most ordinary materials. A fresh wreath can be a sparkling alternative to the dried version; its beauty is fleeting, but the effect is bright. Set a wreath of greens around the base of a pillar candle as a centerpiece, and for napkin rings use small green wreaths, or braided cornhusks twisted into circles.

Dried herb-and-flower swags, wreaths, garlands, and bouquets are treasured for their long-lasting good looks and gentle tones. Use them on tabletops, stairways, and walls. Hang flowers and herbs in a dry, dark attic or closet, or lay them in boxes of cornmeal-and-borax, silica gel, or a similar preserving agent. Dried flowers can be tucked into doilies to make tussie-mussies, or arranged in bouquets. An extreme scale creates the most exciting look: Make bouquets very small or very large. Gather dried fruits and flowers, leaves, pods, and grasses in great bunches, or braid them into decorative door hangings.

Long before detergents and deodorants were commonplace, pomanders

A single variety of dried flower makes a simple but stunning statement. Gather in your hand by the stem, forming the flowers into a rounded shape. When the bouquet is as full as you want, cut the stem ends straight across and insert into a container. Sprays of love-in-a-mist burst from a seventeenth-century brass monteith (opposite). Love-in-a-mist, also known as nigella, is a pod that resembles a rosebud; an annual, it can be air-dried by hanging it upside down. Many craft and floral shops sell it in small bunches.

The best place for a drying rack is a cool, dry room away from direct sunlight (overleaf). Hang small groups of flowers tied with string. You can experiment with different varieties to discover which ones best retain their color and shape.

178

Handmade wreaths can be lushly abundant—dried irises, peonies, and roses hot-glued over Silver King artemisia (above left)—or as utterly simple as clusters of pinecones wired to a frame (above right). A wreath of coiled grapevines is a perpetual racetrack for a toy horse tethered to his wooden rockers (opposite).

kept rooms and people smelling fresh. Pomander-making is a time-honored holday tradition, and a simple one: Stick whole cloves into apples and citrus fruits, then set them to dry in a bowl of spices. The fragrance can be renewed from year to year with a drop or two of essential oil.

The preparation of a craft can become part of your decor. Flowers can be window ornaments when hung to dry, heads down, from a curtain rod. And clove-studded pomanders in a big, glazed bowl scent the room in the process of curing.

Any discussion of nature crafts is incomplete without a nod to the Victorian era, when nature pastimes were wildly popular. Back then, it was not unusual to spend hours encrusting a mirror frame with shells, or drilling holes in individual

It takes a skilled and patient artisan to craft small-scale furniture or create an urn of coiled twigs. The foot-long love seat (opposite) was inspired by turn-of-the-century twig-work furniture, handcrafted of branches pruned from red or white oak trees. The branches are clamped, drilled, and notched, and the twig ends are neatly whittled for a finished look.

To make the sculptural twig urn (above), malleable twigs were soaked, then coiled around a foundation and tacked in place. Placed atop a hickory plant stand, the urn overflows with a mass of waxy magnolia leaves. On the windowsill, two miniature Windsor chairs stand at attention.

pinecone scales before sewing them to silk or paper. When these elaborate creations appear at antiques fairs and estate sales, they are quickly snapped up by eager collectors, who appreciate the time and attention such projects demanded.

The allure of shells is still strong, and though they're not accepted as money anymore, as they were with some Native American peoples, they're still valued for their intriguing shapes, colors, and patterns. Parroting Victorian tradition, you can recall a beach holiday by embellishing flowerpots, lamp shades, wreaths, picture frames, and mirrors with shells. The best time to gather shells is after a storm, when the sea has coughed up new treasures from the deep. A coat of clear acrylic spray or mineral oil keeps the shells shiny. One way to display seashells from a vacation is to make a "sailor's valentine." These booklike shadow boxes, often octagonal in shape, hold pictures created from shells. Sailors made them to pass the time, bringing them home to loved ones as keepsakes from their journeys.

Making crafts out of pinecones is another hobby with roots in the late nineteenth century, when a back-to-nature craze prompted thousands to flee the cities in search of health and vigor. New York State's Adirondack Mountains were a favored destination, where wealthy city folk established lavish "camps" to experience the outdoor life. They returned with pinecone candleholders, fragrant balsam pillows, and other woodsy talismans that reminded them of their forays in the open air. Conjure up your own memories of the outdoors with an armful of fallen oak branches gathered on a neighborhood walk, or a supply of nuts, berries, seeds, and pinecones collected during a summer-long stay in a mountain cabin. Stripping pinecone scales is easy to do with a knife or clippers. Reserve the top "rosettes" to decorate picture frame corners, or glue rosettes side by side on top of a small wooden box.

Twigs with mitered ends form the zigzag embellishment that covers the apron of a pair of twig benches which are stacked to form a simple bookcase (opposite). Made with wood glue and brads, a similar decoration can enliven all sorts of plain wood surfaces, including shelf edges, bedside tables, and porch furniture.

A collection of rustic bentwood rockers illustrates the unique variety of hand-crafted antique furniture (opposite). Highlights of this collection include decorative robin's-egg blue and mustard rockers, and an elaborate Midwestern bird cage from the 1890s. The vintage Adirondack twig picture frame (above) showcases a wonderful scenic landscape. A crosspiece of branches forms the frame, intertwined with a delicate fretwork of fresh or dried-and-soaked vines.

Log beds, twig trim on furniture, twig lamps, and miniatures made of twigs also harken back to the late nineteenth century. Americans expressed their love for the outdoors by making furniture from bark-covered stumps, logs, and sticks. Twig art has revived in recent years, with primitive furniture and accessories adding woodsy relief to our homes. When working with twigs, imagination is paramount. The wood pieces need to be arranged so the shape, texture, and color are pleasing, and the piece must hold together structurally while still retaining its naive originality and wit.

Sometimes the best way to display nature's treasures is to leave them unadorned. Set on a polished tabletop, the beauty of a flat of paperwhites, a bowl of acorns, an abandoned nest, or a gigantic pinecone needs no embellishment.

Experienced crafters can fashion a birch bedstead like this one (opposite), made by a Michigan artist for a lakeside weekend home. The heart-shaped twig headboard (above) is perfect for rooms where nature is part of the decor. The simple bed linens let the headboard take center stage.

Twig blinds aren't operational, but filter the light, mimicking Venetian blinds in a rustic vein. The blinds (left) are easy to make using hot glue and an assortment of thin, straight twigs cut to the exact dimensions of each window with sharp clippers. A pair of thin wires suspends each blind from the top of the window frame. Very long and slender sculptural branches make an impromptu matching valance, courtesy of the great outdoors.

31

A cool, sunny room is an ideal winter sanctuary for fragrant culinary herbs and forced bulbs. In the mudroom (above), fragrant potted herbs spend the cool months of the year in a weathered dry sink, in the same pots in which they summered. Paperwhite narcissus don't require staking if you place them near a window where they will get plenty of sunlight. Old bricks boost pots for better drainage. With a hot glue gun and a great collection of seashells, you can duplicate the look of the shell-encrusted window frame (opposite) and the Victorian-era shell boxes that sit on the twig table. Then create your own museum of natural history by framing distinctive nature specimens in shadow box frames or simply under glass and hanging them on the wall around the window.

Framing a Dried Bouquet

*A shadowbox frame with a mat showcases
a sweet dried bouquet—one of the simplest payoffs
for drying your own flowers.
The flowers may be grown, picked from a friend's garden,
or gathered in open meadows.*

DRYING FLOWERS

Choose flowers or herbs with twiggy stalks and small heads; a list of suggested varieties appears opposite—any of the flowers (except hydrangea and Chinese Lanterns, whose flower or pod heads are too large for this treatment) would be suitable. Hang-drying works best in an attic or other dry, dark, warm, well-ventilated place, but if there's a long period of dry weather, a closet or garage may be used as well. Drying times and color retention will vary according to the site, the climate, and the type of flower.

To begin, strip the leaves from the first few inches of the stems. Tie flowers of the same type together loosely in small bunches with cotton string or twine, leaving the string ends long. Attach these ends to a peg, nail, rafter, clothesline, or other support, so that air can circulate all around the flowers. Let the flowers dry until the petals are papery and the stems are brittle—anywhere from three days to three weeks.

PREPARING THE FRAME

Remove the backing from the frame and add a mat if the frame doesn't have one. Glue a small block of Styrofoam that's the same depth as the frame to the back of the mat in each corner; these spacers will keep the mat pressed against the glass. If you like, glue a special paper—in a particular color or texture—onto the frame backing, smoothing out any air bubbles.

ASSEMBLING THE FRAME

Wrap twine around the center of the stems on the bunch of dried flowers, cinching them in only slightly. Tie the twine ends in a knot behind the bunch and leave the ends long. Center the dried flowers on the frame's backing. Put the mat in place temporarily to make sure the flower heads are inside the mat opening. Then trim the stem ends even with the inside of the frame edge. Use a pencil to mark the position of the twine knot on the backing. Remove the backing and use an awl or other pointed tool to pierce a hole through the backing at the marked position, then make another hole ⅛ inch away. Draw the twine ends through these holes, tie them in a knot on the back, and trim the ends. Place this in the frame and then reassemble the frame.

Florals for Hang-Drying

ARTEMISIA
(Artemisia)

BABY'S BREATH
(Gypsophila)

BACHELOR'S BUTTONS
(Centaurea cyanus)

BLACK-EYED SUSAN
(Rudbeckia)

CHINESE LANTERNS
(Physalis alkekengi)

COCKSCOMB
(Celosia cristata)

EVERLASTINGS
(Xeranthemum)

FEVERFEW
(Chrysanthemum parthenium)

GLOBE AMARANTH
(Gomphrena globosa)

HYDRANGEA
(Hydrangea)

LARKSPUR
(Consolida orientalis)

LAVENDER
(Lavandula)

LOVE-IN-A-MIST
(Nigella damascena)

SALVIA
(Salvia)

STATICE
(Limonium sinuatum)

SWEET ANNIE
(Artemisia)

TANSY
(Tanacetum)

TEA ROSES
(Rosa)

YARROW
(Achillea)

A Wreath of Fresh Flowers

*This pretty decoration begins with just-picked florals,
but ones that will air-dry in place promise
a long-lasting piece. Choose flowers with stems that are
thin and bendable such as the tansy, artemisia,
and goldenrod in this wreath;
then tuck in the scarlet and yellow celosia.*

MATERIALS

18" crimped wire wreath form
or medium-gauge (20-, 24-,
or 28-gauge) wire

Fresh flowers and plants on
long stems

Springs of herbs (optional)

Green florist's spool wire or
thin vines such as
honeysuckle (optional)

TOOLS

Wire cutters

Pliers

FINISHED SIZE:
ABOUT 20" IN DIAMETER

PREPARING THE FORM

A combination of flowers from the garden, wildflowers, and even weeds contribute to the free-spirited look of this wreath. To ensure that the flowers will keep their color over time, pick them just before their peak maturity, in the morning after the dew has dried, and place them in water until you are ready to work with them.

Use a thin wire wreath form as the base or, if one is not available, make a circle about 18 inches in diameter with medium-gauge wire. At the top of the circle, twist the wire ends together and clip off any excess wire. You can also use a wire coat hanger to make the circle, shaping it with pliers to help create a smooth curve.

ASSEMBLING THE WREATH

To assemble the wreath, it's best to work with one type of floral at a time. Beginning with a green or silvery plant material such as artemisia, wrap the stems around the wreath form, covering the wire completely. It is not necessary at this early stage to tuck in the loose ends. Next, attach the flowers by wrapping the stems around the wrapped base. Work with one flower at a time, arranging it so the flower heads extend out from the circle. For celosia or other florals with thick stems, cut each stem to 3 or 4 inches and tuck it in between the spiral wraps of the other stems. You will want to distribute the colors fairly evenly all around the wreath, but an occasional loose piece and a not-quite-perfect circle are ways to create a charmingly uncontrived look.

FINISHING

For added fragrance, you may want to include herbs in the composition. Insert the sprigs of herbs after you have arranged the flowers and stems. To secure all the elements, if you like, wrap thin vines like honeysuckle or a length of spool wire around the finished wreath. To keep the wreath looking its best, hang it in a dry spot away from direct sunlight.

A Simple Twig Planter

This planter has a classic window box shape, but the technique of gluing twigs to a surface can be applied to any container with flat walls. Picture a coffee can filled with fresh flowers, a square gift box exhibiting gourds, or a shoe box displaying a dried flower arrangement.

MATERIALS

Slender branches or twigs, ¼" to ½" thick

A box with flat sides

Hemp, or waxed linen twine

TOOLS

Saw (a hacksaw, coping saw, table saw, scroll saw, or circular saw)

Pruning shears

Hot glue gun and glue sticks

FINISHED SIZE: AS SHOWN, 10" WIDE BY 26" LONG BY 10" HIGH

PREPARING THE BOX AND TWIGS

If necessary, remove the top rim or any decorative molding from the box so the working surface is flat. When choosing a box, note that the planter is designed for indoor or seasonal outdoor use. Hot glue—even hot wood glue, which can be harder to extrude but makes a more durable bond—will crack in freezing temperatures.

Use a saw to cut the twigs 1 inch longer than the height of the box. Use pruning shears to remove any offshoots.

APPLYING THE TWIGS

Cover your work surface with newspaper and place the box on its side on top of this protected surface. Test a twig against the side of the box to determine the twig's flattest surface. Run a bead of hot glue down the center of the twig on its flat side, stopping 1 inch from the top and bottom. Starting at a corner of the box, hold the twig against the wall of the box with 1 inch extending beyond the top edge of the box. Hold the twig for a few seconds until the glue bonds. Test each twig to determine its flattest surface and to see how tightly it will fit alongside a previously glued twig. Pick and choose twigs that will provide a good, tight fit, then glue subsequent twigs in the same manner until the box is covered on all four sides.

LACING THE TOP EDGE

Cut the twine or hemp into 18-inch lengths. At one corner, tie the end of one strand of twine around a twig, 1 inch from the top. Keep the knot at the back and leave a 4-inch tail. To lace, use an overcast wrap as follows: Bring the twine behind the second twig and

TOP VIEW

FRONT VIEW

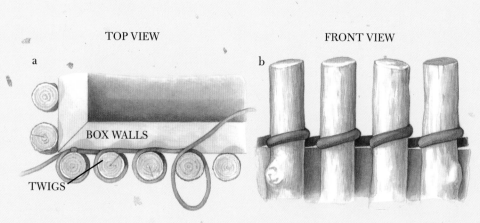

a

BOX WALLS

TWIGS

b

wrap the twine around it, bringing the twine to the front and then around to the back again (a). Bring the twine to the back of the third twig, and then wrap twine around it. Keep the wraps consistent and aligned (b). At the end of a strand of twine, knot another strand onto it, keeping the knot at the back. After the last twig is wrapped, tie the two ends in a knot, and trim the ends of twine.

LACING THE BOTTOM EDGE

Lacing at the bottom edge is a little more difficult than lacing the top edge because the twigs cannot extend an inch below the planter or the weight of the planter would rest on the twigs and not on the foundation box. For the bottom edge, turn the box upside down and lace in the same way as you did for the top edge, this time wedging the twine into the space between the unglued ends of the twigs and the box. Keep the wraps consistent and aligned, moving them into place with a needle if necessary. When the bottom lacing is complete and the twine ends are knotted, squeeze more hot glue into the space between the ends of the twigs and the box to keep the twining in place. Allow the glue to dry.

A Gilded Vine
Ornament

*Imagine lots of vine balls—left natural,
or sprayed with various metallic paint colors—nestled
in a long wood trough. Or decorate the balls to suit the occasion:
Add a sprig of mistletoe to the bow and hang it high
for a kissing ball, or add dried flowers and use as a centerpiece
for a dinner party.*

MATERIALS

Vines that grow upward

Spool of fine brass wire

Gold spray paint

1 yard of 1"-wide ribbon

⅝ yard of wire-edged ombré ribbon

1 package of seed beads or pearls, 3mm

TOOLS

Large washbasin

Cardboard box

Wire cutters

**FINISHED SIZE:
ABOUT 5" IN DIAMETER**

DRYING THE VINES

To recreate Jane Fleischmann's twig ball, use vines that grow upward such as grape, honeysuckle, or morning glory; do not use creeping vines. Strip off the leaves, then let the vines dry until they are brown and brittle. Drying time will vary depending on the type and age of the vine and the humidity, so allow a few days to a few weeks.

FORMING THE BALL

Immerse the dry vines in a basin of lukewarm water for 15 to 30 minutes or until the vines are very pliable. To wind the vines into a ball—a process similar to winding yarn into a ball—begin with a fine end of one vine and wrap it about 6 times around the fingers of one hand. Slip these coils off your fingers, and wrap the vine around them tightly, making the wraps perpendicular to the 6 coils. Wrap as close to the ends as possible but not so close that the wraps slip off, and build up the wraps in the center as high as possible. Then change direction and wrap on one diagonal, then on the other. Once the ball is fairly round, change directions frequently to maintain the round shape.

When you come to the end of a vine, tuck it into a previous wrap, or work over it with the next vine. Continue wrapping until the ball measures about 6 inches across, or the desired diameter. Weave the final few inches of vine under and over a few strands, and then pull it tightly. Tuck the end into the ball, or clip it close to the surface. Allow the ball to dry thoroughly for a few days.

GILDING

Cut an 8-inch strand of wire and slide it under a sturdy strand of vine on the ball. Bring the wire up so it is doubled and twist the ends into a hook. Hang the vine ball by the wire hook on the inside wall of a large cardboard box. Working outside or in a well-ventilated area, spray-paint the ball with the metallic paint. Move the wire to rotate the ball, exposing every side as you paint. Allow the ball to dry for several hours.

FINISHING

Cut a long strand of wire and wrap one end of it around a secure strand of wrapped vine, tucking the wire end inside the ball. Thread the seed beads onto the wire. Wrap the beaded wire around the vine ball a few times, changing direction with each wrap. As you wrap, distribute the beads in small groups along the length of the wire. When you have finished wrapping the wire, twist the wire end around a vine and tuck the end into the ball.

To make a hanging loop, thread one end of the 1-inch-wide ribbon under a wire wrap and under one or two vine wraps. Bring the ribbon ends up even with each other and knot them together at the ends.

To make a decorative bow, thread the wire-edged ribbon through a wire and vine wrap at a point on the ball opposite the hanging loop. Tie the ribbon in a bow, arrange the loops and tails attractively, then trim the ribbon ends on the diagonal. Also trim the ends of the hanging loop.

A Fresh Lemon Topiary

A fresh lemon topiary in a moss-covered clay pot adds fragrance as well as natural good looks to any table setting. The frosted pinecones lighten the overall effect and help to create a gracious centerpiece like those often seen in historical restorations.

MATERIALS

Clay flowerpot, 8" in diameter by 6" high

24"-tall cone of Styrofoam or green plastic foam

⅔ yard of chicken wire (galvanized steel hexagonal mesh) with ½" to 1" holes

Newspaper

Small amount of sphagnum moss

36–40 lemons

24 small pinecones

24 wood floral picks with wires

White paint

Floral picks or sturdy toothpicks

Several sprigs of leafy evergreens on woody stems such as laurel (shown), boxwood, or rhododendron

TOOLS

Wire cutters

Pliers

Hot glue gun and glue sticks

Small paintbrush

FINISHED SIZE: ABOUT 24" TALL

MAKING THE FOUNDATION

To make a topiary similar to Debbie Roub's, center the cone in the pot and glue it in place with the hot glue gun. Wrap the chicken wire around the cone. Use wire cutters to clip the excess wire, and use pliers to wrap the wire ends to secure the overlap. Push wads of tightly balled up newspaper into the pot between the cone and the pot, and hot-glue them to create a firm base.

EMBELLISHING

Working on one small area at a time, apply hot glue to the outside of the pot. Immediately pick up clumps of moss with pliers, tweezers, or tongs and press them into hot glue. Cover the entire pot with moss in this way.

Attach a wood floral pick with wires to each pinecone by wrapping the wire around the cone's bottom round of "petals." To give each pinecone a frosted look, paint the tips of each petal with white paint. If you like, at crafts stores you can purchase pinecones with picks already attached.

FLORAL ARRANGING

Reserve a small, round, unblemished lemon for the top of the topiary. With the other lemons, insert the pointy end of a floral pick (or toothpick) into the center of one side of each lemon and push the opposite end of the pick into the cone. Begin with the largest lemons at the bottom and work up the cone in rounds of lemons of decreasing size; make sure you keep the lemons vertical. Space the lemons in each round about ½ inch apart, but keep the rounds close together, staggering the lemons so their pointed ends fit into the space between the lemons in the row below. At the top, when there is no room left for another round, mash down the tip of the foam cone so it is flat. Insert a pick in the flatter end of the reserved lemon and push the opposite end of the pick into the center top of the cone.

Cut the evergreen leaves into small sprigs with 2-inch-long stems. Fill in the areas between the lemons, alternating leafy sprigs and pinecones. At the bottom, insert more moss. If necessary, hot-glue moss in between the lemons so that the foundation cone does not show.

Place the topiary in a dry location away from direct sunlight. Many of the lemons will air-dry, but some will not. Check daily and replace any lemons that get moldy.

A Cookie Garland and a Pomander

MATERIALS

GARLAND:

3 gingerbread cookies

4 freeze-dried orange slices

Clear acrylic spray sealer

8 red wooden ball beads, 12mm

1 yard ⅝"-wide flat ribbon

Red thread

POMANDER:

Orange

Whole cloves

Powdered orrisroot,
    1 tablespoon per pomander

1 tablespoon each ground
    cinnamon, ground nutmeg,
    and/or ground cloves
    (optional)

TOOLS

GARLAND:

Gingerbread cookie cutter

Hot glue gun and glue sticks

Sewing or embroidery needle

POMANDER:

Grease pencil

Awl, thin knitting needle,
    compass tip, or other
    pointed object

**FINISHED SIZE: GARLAND,
ABOUT 30" LONG**

Crafts made from food mean spending time in the kitchen, the true heart of any home. Making gingerbread cookies, an old European culinary craft, and pomanders, wonderful room fresheners, means a kitchen that resonates with luscious smells and lively conversation.

PREPARING THE GARLAND

For a garland like the one by Judy Divelbiss, make a batch of gingerbread cookies, using either of the recipes on page 47. Choose the three best shapes to use in the garland. To prolong the life of the garland, use a spray sealer in a well-ventilated area to lightly coat the cookies, beads, and orange slices.

ASSEMBLING THE GARLAND

Lay the ribbon out flat on a clean work surface. Place the gingerbread cookies along the ribbon, with a freeze-dried orange slice in between and at either end of the cookies. Place a wooden bead on either side of each orange slice. Make sure the middle gingerbread cookie is centered on the ribbon, then tighten the spacing so all the elements are close together, with an equal amount of ribbon at each end. Hot-glue the gingerbread cookies and orange slices in position on the ribbon. Thread a sewing needle and sew the beads in place. Tie a loop in the ribbon close to each end and display the garland by hanging these loops on a small hook or nail that has been hammered into the wall.

PREPARING THE ORANGE

Wash and dry the orange for the pomander. Use a grease pencil to draw a simple design. To recreate the design shown in the photograph, mark freehand a line from the stem end to the opposite end of the orange. Draw a second line perpendicular to it, crossing the first line at the center, like an equator. Mark two points on the vertical line, each ¾ inch from the center; then mark two points along the horizontal line, each 1¼ inches from the center. Connect these points to form a diamond. Use a paper towel to rub off the marked lines inside the diamond. In the photograph, the pomander is studded only on the front, but you can create the same design on the opposite side of the orange if you like.

If the pomander is to hang in a closet, you will need a piece of narrow, ⅜-inch-wide ribbon that is long enough to both wrap around the orange and form a hanging loop. Start by wrapping the ribbon around the orange first, then draw a design that includes the ribbon. The cloves inserted in the orange will also secure the ribbon.

Oranges are best-loved for pomanders because of their fragrance, shape, and color, but any citrus fruit as well as apples may be used. Pomanders can be completely studded with cloves or they can be decorated with a simple motif.

INSERTING THE CLOVES

Sort through the whole cloves and set aside those without stems for a cooking project. Push the stem of each clove into the orange along the outlines drawn. Keep the cloves about ⅛ inch apart; as the orange dries, this space will shrink. If the rind of the orange is particularly hard, or the end of the clove is blunt, insert a sharp, pointed object such as a compass tip into the orange first to make a pilot hole for the clove. When the outline is completely studded, fill in the diamond with cloves by making one or more rows of concentric cloves or by adding a random sprinkling of cloves.

FINISHING THE POMANDER

To preserve the pomander, roll it in a mixture of powdered orrisroot, available at a craft or health food store, and spices from the grocery store. Orrisroot is a preservative which will protect the pomander against mold and the spices provide additional scent to the mixture.

Mix the orrisroot and optional spices in a shallow bowl. Roll the studded fruit in the bowl and use your fingers to sprinkle and rub the powder mixture over the orange, getting the mixture into the pierced areas. Place the finished pomander in a dry location away from direct sunlight.

Two Recipes for Gingerbread Cookies

Making gingerbread cookies is always enjoyable because the cookies are delicious

to eat as well as fun to include in decorating projects.

If you make the edible cookies, you'll want to make extra so everyone

can have a taste. For a more durable decoration,

you can make the inedible cookies.

REAL DOUGH GINGERBREAD COOKIES

MAKES ABOUT 15 COOKIES

2⅓ cups sifted all-purpose flour

½ cup sugar

⅛ teaspoon baking soda

1 teaspoon ground ginger

¼ teaspoon ground nutmeg

¼ teaspoon ground cinnamon

¼ teaspoon salt

½ cup soft shortening

½ cup dark molasses

¼ cup raisins

1. Sift the first seven ingredients together into a large bowl. Add the shortening. With a pastry blender or two knives, cut the shortening into the flour mixture until the mixture resembles very coarse crumbs.

2. Gradually stir in the molasses. Work the dough in the bowl with lightly floured fingers until the mixture is well blended. Chill in the refrigerator for at least 1 hour.

3. Heat the oven to 375°F. Grease the baking sheets and set them aside.

4. Place half the dough on a well-floured surface and pat it into a rectangle. Place a sheet of floured waxed paper over the dough, and roll it out to a thickness of ¼ inch. Remove the waxed paper. Repeat with the second half of the dough.

5. Cut out shapes using a cookie cutter. Use a spatula to transfer the cutouts onto a greased baking sheet. Press raisins into each cookie for the eyes and buttons. Bake the cookies for 7 minutes or until nicely browned. Cool the cookies on the baking sheet for 2 minutes, then remove them to wire racks to cool completely.

PLAY DOUGH GINGERBREAD COOKIES

MAKES ABOUT 5 LARGE SHAPES

½ cup all-purpose flour

½ cup cornstarch

½ cup white craft glue

red and green food coloring

½ teaspoon ground cinnamon

¼ teaspoon ground ginger

¼ cup raisins

1. Mix the flour and cornstarch together in a bowl. Remove a small portion of this mixture and set it aside. Add the glue to the remaining mixture and stir. The mixture will look like moist crumbs.

2. Using your fingers, knead the mixture evenly until the dough forms a small ball. (This will take about 10 minutes.) If dough is too stiff, add a little water. If dough is too moist or sticky, add more of the flour-and-cornstarch mixture.

If dough does not attain a workable elasticity, wrap it in plastic wrap and let it set for a couple of days. When you work with it again, you may need to add a bit more flour and cornstarch. At this point, tint the dough brown using several drops of red and green food coloring. For the aroma of real cookies, you can add the spices.

3. Roll out the dough between two layers of wax paper. Cut out shapes with a cookie cutter. Press raisins in place for the eyes and buttons. Allow the shapes to dry in a cool, dry place until the front of the cookies is hard and dry—at least 24 hours and often as long as 3 days. Then turn the shapes over and allow the backs to dry.

A Fall Wreath of
~ Dried Flowers ~

*A dried flower wreath, a harbinger of autumn,
is a reminder of a garden's bounty. Gather pink and blue
hydrangeas just before their peak color; they darken somewhat
as they dry. Bittersweet, or celastrus, is a vine that
often grows rampant along roadsides.*

MATERIALS

18" grapevine wreath,
  purchased or homemade

Florist's spool wire

Stub wire

8 fresh or dried hydrangea
  blossoms

2 large or 5 small branches of
  bittersweet

3 white miniature pumpkins,
  varnished

Varnish (optional)

TOOLS

Wire cutter

Hot glue gun and glue sticks

Small foam brush for applying
  varnish (optional)

FINISHED SIZE: ABOUT 20"
IN DIAMETER

MAKING A VINE WREATH

To make a vine wreath like this one by James Cramer, gather grapevines, honeysuckle, forsythia, or long, thin branches of any woody plant. Strip the leaves from the vines. While the vines are still green and pliable, form them into a circle, twisting and wrapping the strands around each other. Build up the wreath to the desired thickness. If necessary, use a little florist's wire to secure the vines in a few places. Set the wreath aside and let it dry completely.

CREATING A HANGING LOOP

To make a hanging loop, wrap stub wire or several strands of spool wire around a few sturdy vines on the top back of the wreath. Make a loop, then secure the wire at a point about 3 inches away. Return to the original place and twist the wire ends together.

PREPARING THE ELEMENTS

Hydrangea and bittersweet can be used fresh because they air-dry in place nicely. Keep the leaves intact on both. Miniature pumpkins are often sold with a sealer finish, but if yours do not have one and you want

the pumpkins to last longer, apply two coats of varnish to each, letting them dry thoroughly after each coat.

ARRANGING THE FLORALS

It's best to work with one type of floral at a time. Begin with the hydrangea; trim the stems to 6 inches. Spacing the blooms unevenly, insert the stems into the wreath and hot glue them. If the branches of bittersweet are long, begin at the top of the wreath and wrap the branches around the wreath, letting each branch cover about half the wreath. Allow the branch vines to spiral around the hydrangea and try to keep the large berry clusters at the front. Insert any offshoots into the wreath and hot glue them sparingly.

If the bittersweet comes in small sprigs, distribute them all around, inserting the stems into the wreath. Secure them with spool wire or hot glue.

Decide where you want the miniature pumpkins to be. The most secure places are gaps where at least two thick vines provide a flat base. Apply hot glue very generously to the bottom of each pumpkin and immediately press it into position on the vines.

artistry with
PAPER

No matter how advanced, how computerized our society becomes, there will always be paper. Love letters, old photographs, theater tickets, drawings, postcards, newspaper articles, recipe cards, poetry—nothing holds a memory like these paper tokens, each one a piece of the past.

Capture pretty wallpaper in a gilded frame and use it to kindle a touching still life (opposite) complete with flowery mementos gathered on the dresser. The small collage (right) reveals the potential of postage stamps; the frame is wrapped with colorful marbleized paper; you can find it at art supply stores, or make it yourself by floating ink over a mixture of oil and water, and then laying the paper on top.

Many paper crafts from days gone by are still enjoyed today because of the enduring pleasures they bring, not only to those who make the items, but to those who admire the finished results. Colorful postage stamps, shiny catalogue pages, wrapping papers, food boxes,

paper bags, and the print linings of envelopes are all wonderful fodder for a host of paper crafts, many of them modern-day interpretations of techniques that are centuries old. Paper has always inspired the senses. It is beautiful to look at, feel, and smell. It can be folded, framed, cut, or arranged in a collage to best enjoy its beauty. As with any artistic endeavor, the enjoyment is in the process, not just the result.

Paper was made by the early Egyptians from slices of papyrus reeds crisscrossed in layers and smoothed with stone. The Chinese used paper for clothing and wrapping, but their early efforts weren't smooth enough to write on. They also mixed paper scraps with glue to make an early form of papier-mâché (which means "chewed paper" in French), and crafted it into boxes and trays. Vellum, made of calf or lamb gut, and parchment, made from sheep and goat skin, were the forerunners of today's wood-pulp paper. The first paper mill in America began operating near Philadelphia in 1690, and though paper was scarce in Colonial times, there was always enough pretty paper to cut a border for a shelf, or newspaper with which to line a hatbox.

Paper-covered hatboxes and the decorative bandboxes that stored fresh shirt collars are no longer daily necessities, yet their charm persists. Antique boxes are sought after by collectors, and many contemporary versions are mass-produced to imitate their wallpaper-covered cousins of the past. In the early 1800s, wallpaper manufacturers advertised their wares by imprinting wallpaper-covered boxes with the company name and selling them for a few cents each as handy storage containers. They also printed wallpaper in the shape of oval or round storage boxes, and sold it to the creative do-it-yourselfers of those days. These antique boxes covered in pretty wrapping paper, marbleized paper, patterned endpapers, or dainty wallpaper evoke the aura of yesteryear.

At its best, decoupage is improvised and freeform with images cut from garden catalogues, wrapping paper, and old books. Seal a decoupaged tabletop with many coats of polyurethane or varnish to make it durable and easy to clean. Cutting out the fine stems for the decoupage (opposite) requires patience and nimble fingers. Adding three-dimensional elements such as silk leaves and a paper-lace cuff with buttons makes this an out-of-the-ordinary work of art. It's fun to copy a famous print; this one is loosely based on "Rosa centifolia," by the nineteenth-century French painter Henri "Le Douanier" Rousseau.

Quillwork is a whimsical paper craft that was a fad with Colonial schoolgirls in eighteenth-century America. Wrapping thin strips of paper around a toothpick or thin stick (or a bird feather, hence the name) created coils, spirals, and rolls. The paper coils were then glued down to form intricate designs. In thirteenth-century Europe, rolled coils of paper with gilded edges cut from Bibles imitated jewelry filigreed with lacelike ornamental silver wire or fine gold. By the seventeenth century, nuns were using quillwork to embellish medallions, crosses, and other religious articles. Quillwork was sometimes combined with beads, shells, and metallic threads to decorate the back plates of Victorian sconces and to make intricate floral pictures. It is still a creative pastime for both children and adults, and precut paper ready to roll is available at craft stores.

Scrapbooks are a lovely way to lasso treasured bits of paper. Years ago, young ladies would spend leisurely hours with a glue pot and scissors arranging memories in personal albums, created as pictorial diaries and fondly consulted in later years as a record of the past. Making a scrapbook remains an enjoyable pastime for anyone with a desire to collect and preserve the past.

Decoupage, from the French word *découper* (to cut out) is the art of covering a surface with glued paper cutouts. Eighteenth-century French and Italians first took to decoupage in an attempt to imitate Japanese lacquered furniture. Decoupage has a childlike essence: cutting out pretty pictures with scissors and gluing them to something else. The freedom and creativity of decoupage makes it one of the most accessible paper crafts, drawing many to the art.

Valentines, snowflakes, and paper-lace shelf trim are just some of the items you can make with cut paper. This rich folk tradition hails from many countries, especially those in Asia, where working with paper is a fine art. Sentimental

Serendipitous and whimsical, a collage blends disparate elements into one harmonious composition. Auction catalogues and decorating magazines often yield suitable images, like the blue-and-white Staffordshire china (above) or the delicate antique furniture (opposite), combined, in this case, with postage stamps to create miniature renderings. Sharp scissors and rubber cement are the simple tools of this imaginative hobby.

To replicate these nineteenth-century storage boxes (left and above), find large papier-mâché and cardboard boxes at craft stores. Cover them with wallpaper and line them with newspaper. Search out vintage papers at flea markets; to strengthen the paper against tears, spray it with several light coats of acrylic sealer before starting the project. For other old-fashioned looks, use a combination of new wallpapers that look antique, apply wallpaper cutouts decoupage-style, or stencil the box with a vintage design.

paper-cuts were all the rage during the eighteenth and early nineteenth centuries. As a parlor pastime, Victorian ladies transferred lacy designs to paper. The same effect is imitated by today's creative shelf trims made from kraft paper, newspaper, or shiny white paper cut with graphic designs such as schoolhouses, pine trees, hearts, and diamonds. These cut papers often look like quilt patterns or have the simplicity of Pennsylvania Dutch designs.

Silhouettes, or shadow portraits, are among the most charming paper crafts, evoking instant nostalgia. Silhouettes are usually cut by hand, sometimes by machine, with the cutout mounted on contrasting paper for best effect.

At one time these paper outlines of people's heads were regarded with derision. Some people considered the silhouette a meager substitute for expensive oil portraits or miniatures. The name of Etienne de Silhouette, Louis XV's minister of finance, is immortalized by the craft. It is unclear whether this was because he was an avid silhouette cutter, as some claim, or whether he was simply being mocked when his name became associated with the craft of "empty" drawings after he attempted to reduce the pensions of the French nobility.

Silhouettes had a century-long heyday beginning in middle of the eighteenth century in Europe, England, and America. At the end of the 1800s, a scientific movement led by Charles Darwin's stepcousin claimed a person's character was revealed by the outlines of his or her face, and silhouettes were sometimes used to bolster the theory. They fell from favor as photography progressed. Today, silhouettes can be an interesting alternative to a photographic portrait.

Collage is a serendipitous craft. The heart of this art form is spontaneous playfulness. Scraps of paper, taken out of context, are rearranged to form scenes of excitement and surprise. With collage, improvisation reigns.

Artful groups of similar items give a collection added impact. The silhouettes (opposite) are hung in multiples and set off by the light and dark fireplace wall of this Connecticut bedroom. Antique silhouettes are highly collectible and should be professionally framed to protect them from deterioration. A hand-painted paper shade (above) adorns an iron table lamp. Shade-making kits are available at craft stores, or search out aging shades at antique shops, strip off the old fabric, and use the frame as the basis for a new shade. Then hand-paint the shade using acrylic paints or watercolors. To avoid singeing a paper shade of this size, always pair it with a low-wattage bulb.

Shelf trim dresses up open shelves, a Welsh dresser, or the inside of a hutch or cupboard. Making the trim yourself adds a warm handmade note to the decor. In the kitchen (opposite), simple brown kraft paper lines the shelves of a jelly cupboard found at a flea market; the edge of the paper is folded down and decorated with a repeating schoolhouse motif. Because the doors of the cupboard are usually open, the trim is admired daily. Make the silhouette from a precut stencil, a potato print, or a rubber stamp. For a fancier look, use paper lace to add a frilly trim to pantry shelves (above); the white lace sets off the ironstone and sprigged china on display. Rubber cement is a fine temporary bond for any shelf trim. Replace the trim and shelf paper every few months to keep it looking fresh.

Surround your favorite print with a beveled mat made with a special tool sold at framing stores and art suppliers. Interesting frames found at tag sales, flea markets, estate sales, and auctions can be gilded, painted, or stained. The flowery design of an 1850 Pennsylvania fraktur (opposite) is echoed by the fresh-picked bouquet below it. People and puppies are the subjects of an eclectic grouping in the cozy den (above left). Connections between similar objects can be set up by displaying them side by side. The owner of the Indian Bonnet lustre-ware tea set (below left) figured out its probable vintage when she noticed the same hues and patterns in Joseph Davis's 1836 watercolor of a young girl.

A Decoupage Serving Tray

Decoupage is the art of applying cutout images to a surface and then protecting it with several layers of varnish, making the item look like it has been hand-painted. This decoupage tray exudes spring with its birds and flowers.

MATERIALS

A wooden tray

Floral images

Clear acrylic spray

Primer

Acrylic paint in teal or desired color

#120-grit sandpaper

Decoupage medium

Water-based varnish

Masking tape

TOOLS

Flat foam paintbrushes, ½" and 1" wide

Small, sharp scissors

Small brayer (optional)

Tack cloth

FINISHED SIZE: AS SHOWN, 13½" BY 18"

PREPARING THE TRAY

To make a tray similar to Richard Kollath's design, cover your work surface. Sand the tray smooth and wipe it clean with a dust cloth.

If the chosen images are thin, old, or fragile, extend their durability by spraying them with a light coat of acrylic sealer. Work outside, if possible, or in a well-ventilated area and place the papers in a large cardboard box to contain the overspray. Allow the papers to dry before using them.

PAINTING

To apply the primer and paint to the tray, use a 1-inch foam brush and work with the grain of the wood. Work on the underside first, let it dry, then work on the top surface.

To begin, prime all the surfaces and allow the tray to dry thoroughly. Apply a thin coat of paint. Allow the tray to dry thoroughly again, then sand it lightly and wipe it with a dust cloth. Apply one or two more coats of paint, sanding lightly in between each coat, until the color is completely opaque and covers the wood. Let the tray dry completely before applying the images.

THE DECOUPAGE

Using small, sharp scissors, cut out the images. Turn the paper, not the scissors, as you work to ensure maximum control of the fine movement. If this is your first decoupage project, for ease in cutting and gluing choose large, full shapes rather than ones with slender stems or tendrils.

Arrange the images on the tray and keep them in place with small pieces of masking tape. Using the smaller foam brush, apply a thin coat of decoupage medium to the wrong side of each image, then reposition it on the tray. To secure the images and to push out air bubbles, roll them with a brayer or simply smooth them with your fingers. Allow the images to dry thoroughly.

FINISHING

Use a foam brush to apply at least two coats of varnish, allowing the surface to dry thoroughly between coats. Sand the tray lightly and wipe clean with a tack cloth. After the final coat of varnish has dried, wait a few days to let the tray "cure" before handling it or placing any objects on it.

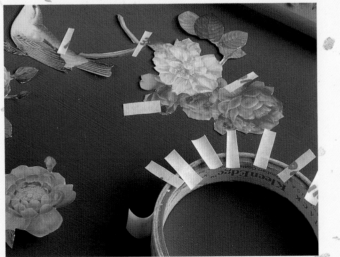

Scherenschnitte
~ Shelf Edging ~

Scherenschnitte, or scissors-cutting, brought to the New World by German immigrants who settled in Pennsylvania in the seventeenth century, is a way of creating intricate paper designs that were used originally to embellish marriage and birth certificates, house blessings, and valentines. Scherenschnitte patterns snipped out of newspaper create a poor man's lace that gives a humble charm to a border.

PLANNING THE BORDER

In this design, the newspaper extends to the back of the shelf, becoming both shelf liner and edging. To begin, measure the width and depth of each shelf to be lined and edged. Then add 3½ inches to the depth measurement for the border.

Use a pencil and ruler to mark these dimensions on the classified pages of a newspaper; keep the columns vertical so in the finished shelf liner the scalloped edge of the border will fall on the blank white margin at the top or bottom of the newspaper page. Cut out the shape and test its fit. Trim as necessary so the paper lies flat on the shelf and the paper edge hangs freely over the edge of the shelf.

CUTTING THE DESIGNS

Trace the actual-size patterns on page 69 onto tracing paper. Work along the area designated for the overhang and use two or more layers of paper at a time, if you like, to make the work go faster. Use the bottom edge of the columns of text as a baseline to keep the cutout designs straight. For each half pattern, fold the newspaper once along the margin between columns or along the middle of a column, depending on where you want the design to be. Make a crease that is about 5 inches deep. Position the tracing of the pattern on top of the newspaper with the dashed lines along the fold. Put paper clips above and below the pattern motif to secure it. Cut along the marked lines. For each quarter pattern, work on only one piece of newspaper at a time. Fold the paper in half vertically the same as for the half patterns, then fold the paper again horizontally, centering the fold in the overhang area. Position the tracing of the motif on the newspaper, matching the dashed lines to folds. Cut out the design. Use a hole punch for the small circular cutouts. Vary the motifs and space them approximately 1 or 2 inches apart. With a little practice, you may want to cut out your own designs freehand.

The deep border of this newspaper shelf edging more than accommodates a variety of folk images such as a heart, a house, trees, and simple geometric shapes. The scalloped edge is easy to cut and adds a graceful finishing touch.

FINISHING

Layer two or more of the cut-paper shelf edgings together, and place the tracing of the repeat pattern for the scalloped edge along the bottom edge; paper clip it in place. Cut along the marked line. Move the pattern as necessary and repeat the pattern across the length of the shelf edging.

To eliminate the creases formed by folding the newspaper, iron it: Set a dry iron to a hot setting. Place a paper towel over the newspaper above and below the cut shapes and press the creases for a few seconds.

VARIATIONS

These same folk art images could be cut out of a variety of papers to create an entirely different look. Try using brown kraft paper, butcher paper, sturdy gift wrapping paper, or even an interestingly textured paper available from an art supply store.

You could change the style of the shelf lining by repeating only one or two images. Try repeating the heart and a small geometric shape for shelf lining for a linen closet, or use a repeat of the trees and house for the shelves in a child's bedroom.

Patterns for the Shelf Edging

ACTUAL-SIZE HALF PATTERNS

ACTUAL-SIZE QUARTER PATTERNS

ACTUAL-SIZE REPEAT PATTERN FOR THE SCALLOPED EDGE

A Portrait in Silhouette

The art of creating silhouettes was a popular pastime in an era before cameras were in widespread use—silhouettes were the snapshots of their day. Making a white silhouette on a black background is a nice change from the more traditional black silhouette on a white background.

MATERIALS

Thin white paper such as lightweight bond typing paper or photocopy paper

Masking tape

Good-quality white matte-finish paper

Heavyweight, black matte-finish, untextured paper such as bristol board, mat board, poster board, or illustration board

Rubber cement

Frame

Mat with an oval opening (optional)

TOOLS

Slide projector or flashlight

Pencil

Ultra-fine felt tip permanent ink marking pen

Stapler

Small, sharp scissors

SETTING UP

Place a backless stool or a chair about 3 feet in front of a blank wall. Set up a slide projector or prop up a flashlight so the light will be at the same height as the subject's head. Have the person sit comfortably with the face and body in profile and with the chin lifted. When tracing and cutting out the profile, be sure to include some area around the neckline, such as a collar, a bow tie, or the slope of the chest.

TRACING THE SHADOW

Work in a darkened room, if possible. Shine the light on the person's head. To avoid distortion, adjust the height of the light source so the profile is on the same horizontal plane as its shadow. Tape a piece of thin white paper on the wall where the shadow appears and trace around the outline of the shadow with a sharpened pencil.

PHOTOCOPYING AND CUTTING

Trace over the outline with a felt-tip marker. Photocopy the drawing, reducing or enlarging it according to the size you want the finished silhouette to be. It is much easier to cut out a larger profile, so don't make the image too small.

Place the good-quality white paper for the silhouette behind the photocopy and staple around the profile through both papers. Using small, sharp scissors, cut out the profile, cutting through both layers of paper.

FINISHING

Cut the heavyweight paper for the background to the size you want the finished piece to be. To mount the silhouette, put small dabs of rubber cement on the wrong side of the silhouette and position it carefully, centering it on the background. If you like, add an oval mat in a color to match the silhouette. Place a piece of glass on top and frame the finished piece.

If you prefer to make a black silhouette, purchase a piece of good-quality paper in black for the silhouette and the heavyweight mat board in white for the background. Follow the directions, but cut the silhouette out of the black and mount it on white.

Stamp Art
Collage Scenes

Stamps are the predominant but not the only images in these folk art pieces. The engraved stamps have a depth of detail that adds a special quality to the designs. Searching for just the right images to bring to a piece is part of the enjoyment of collage.

MATERIALS

11"-by-14" piece of ragboard

Assorted paper images such as stamps, canceled and unused, cutouts from magazines and prints, stationery edging

An envelope flap

Rubber cement

Spray adhesive

TOOLS

Small, sharp scissors

Craft knife #1

Metal-edged ruler

Cutting mat

FINISHED SIZE: 11" BY 14"

PREPARING

To collect the images, stamp and collectible stores often have bins of canceled stamps. To begin, lay the background board on a work surface in an area free of drafts. To cut the images, use small scissors. To cut any long, straight lines use a craft knife, a metal-edged ruler, and a cutting mat. To create these scenes, collage artist Barbara Braman laid out the images on hand, and tried out different compositions. Even when she was satisfied with the effect, she left it out for a while—for days or even weeks. Each time she walked past it, she made subtle changes or rearrangements. Only after she felt it was ready did she make it permanent with rubber cement. Such unhurried experimentation is the key to a successful composition.

GLUING

To glue images, apply the backgrounds first, then layer on the details, in an order similar to the one described below. Brush the rubber cement onto the large pieces and then reposition them. For small pieces, or edges that have a tendency to come up, apply rubber cement to the edge of an envelope flap. Slide the flap, cement side up, under the cut image, then slide it out and press the image to the background.

ASSEMBLING

The collage artist calls the design opposite *A Gentleman Comes to Call*. To create a similar one, choose a decorative drawer liner for the background wallpaper and mount it onto illustration or ragboard with spray adhesive; then cut out a diamond-shaped window with a craft knife.

The following is a list of the images used in the piece and a source for the image:

Marble floor: marbleized paper from an envelope liner

Window frame and baseboard: striped gift wrapping paper, mitered for the frame

View out the window: a magazine advertisement covered with cellophane wrap

Lady, gentleman, and chair: separate prints from an old book

Side tables, china, and ceiling border: images from a decorating magazine

Lighthouse pictures, doilies, roses in pitcher and ceiling ornament: postage stamps

Nail heads holding up the pictures: hole-punched dots of gold paper

The artist has given the title *Lady at the Staircase* to the stamp collage above. To create a similar one, start with cream-colored ragboard. The following is a list of the images in the collage and a source for them:

Plaid background for rug: liner on opaque double-stick tape

Needlepoint flowers on rug: Whole stamps and cutout stamps

Throw pillow: strip of plaid liner with shell cut from a stamp

View out the window: picture from a magazine with a cutout sailboat added

Window: photocopied from a decorating magazine once on white paper, then the panes were cut out; photocopied once on pale blue paper for the curtain only

Rope swag over valance: a place card

Fresco panels on the wall and the stairs: images photocopied in multiple from a decorating magazine

Staircase: cut from a party invitation

Lady: cut from a print

Chairs: images from a decorating magazine

Topiaries and pots: cut from dark green and brown old postage stamps

Ceiling border and the ribbon ornament: embossed gold paper

Ribbon hangers for the pictures: a decorating magazine

Pictures on the wall: stamps

FINISHING

To complete the collage, frame it or have it professionally framed. Including a mat adds depth and a sense of importance to the collage. Nonglare glass may be used in the frame, but the collage should be hung away from direct sunlight, which would fade the images over time.

Sources for Paper Motifs for Decoupage, Collage, and Other Paper Projects

Collecting paper for decoupage and collage projects, and for covering boxes

can be almost as enjoyable a pursuit as making the project.

The search can become an ongoing treasure hunt that in itself is a delightful pastime.

Any paper that can be cut up is a possibility for collage work, and if the paper is part of a book or very valuable, it can be photocopied and then cut up. Photocopying an image allows you to enlarge or reduce it as much as needed to suit the project you are making.

Mail-order catalogues are a great source for images of all kinds; the catalogues can be from garden nurseries, of antique collections, and from current gift stores.

Gift wrap is another wonderful source for images to be used for decoupage or collage. If an image on a greeting card or postcard appeals to you, it can be used despite its thick paper; simply use a single-edge razor blade to carefully peel away the excess layers of paper.

If the finished item is to be a gift, as you collect the images, look for any motifs that have special meaning and appeal for the intended recipient. Books can be a great source for these. For example, botanical books have wonderful florals and Audubon books have both birds and florals.

When gathering paper to cover a box, look for papers with vintage charm; attics, tag sales, and flea markets may turn up some wonderful rolls of vintage wallpaper. Also try wallpaper stores for end-of-roll pieces, inexpensive discontinued designs, and wallpaper sample books, which have sheets large enough to cover a small box. Old boxes are often lined with newspaper, and thinner papers such as newspaper are great to use where an occasional wrinkle won't be so noticeable.

The following list includes familiar and not-so-familiar sources for paper images that can be used for a variety of projects.

- **gift wrap**
- **gift tags**
- **wallpaper**
- **valentine cards**
- **catalogues**
- **advertising circulars**
- **glossy magazines**
- **paper place mats**
- **art prints**
- **ephemera or vintage collectible papers such as old advertisements, magazines, or postcards**
- **old letters and envelopes (for the script)**
- **sheet music**
- **postage stamps**
- **photographs**
- **color photocopies made from prints or books**
- **vintage photographs or photocopies of them**
- **hand-colored black-and-white photocopies of pictures**
- **color photocopies of fabric**
- **origami paper, rice paper, or other special papers**
- **maps**
- **postcards**
- **greeting cards**
- **cigar bands**
- **packaging of household products**
- **place cards**
- **stationery**
- **the lining of fancy envelopes**
- **a child's drawing**
- **engravings from old books for which the copyright has expired**
- **an old composition from elementary school (for the script)**
- **published collections of decoupage motifs**

Beautiful Bandboxes

MATERIALS

Wallpaper

Lidded box of chipboard or papier-mâché

Rubber cement

Newspaper or gift wrap for liner (optional)

TOOLS

Pencil

Scissors

Cloth tape measure

Metal-edge ruler

Craft knife #1 (optional)

Cutting mat (optional)

a

b

Bandboxes, once used to hold collar bands and other treasures, were the shopping bags of their day. Used both at home or when traveling, the boxes were made of wood or pasteboard and covered with wallpaper—still the best material for applying to the box.

PREPARING AND CUTTING

Choose a box with a loosely fitting lid (to accommodate the paper covering). Plan where the motifs or pattern in the paper will fall before marking and cutting the pieces. Place the box bottom and the lid on the wrong side of the wallpaper. Trace around the shapes lightly in pencil. Use scissors to cut out the curved shapes, leaving a ½-inch margin around the lid piece. Cut the bottom piece just inside the pencil line.

Measure the height and circumference of the box and the lid with a cloth tape measure. Mark strips with these dimensions plus ½-inch margins on each side. Cut out these rectangular strips with a craft knife, metal-edge ruler, and cutting mat. Make notches at ½-inch intervals; to do this, cut out a narrow triangle with its tip just inside the pencil line. Notch both long edges of the

c

box strip, what will be the bottom long edge of the lid strip, and the lid center piece.

COVERING THE BOX

To cover the sides, fold under ¼ inch along one short end of the strip. Apply rubber cement to the wrong side of the strip. Place the other short end at an existing seam on the box or wherever the join will be least noticeable. Press the paper into place, overlapping the folded edge on top of the beginning edge (a). Fold in the tabs on the top and bottom edges. Glue on the bottom piece.

COVERING THE LID

Cover the top of the lid first, folding down the tabs (b). Fold under ¼ inch on the long unnotched edge of the side strip. Apply glue to the wrong side of the strip, press into place, and fold the tabs to the inside (c).

If a lining is desired, use lightweight wallpaper, gift wrap, or newspaper. Trace and cut pieces identical to the traced shapes for the outside, trimming the shapes as necessary to fit inside the box and lid.

at home with
PAINT

Paint has punch, and the power to transform surfaces large and small. It's one of the fastest, easiest, and least expensive ways to change the look of a room. Our ancestors had to mix berries, milk, and walnut oils to turn out a proper paint, but today's computers can copy any color and create a matching paint instantly.

A maple leaf from the yard of a Wisconsin inn provided the image for the stenciled stairs and floor (opposite); the foyer is gaily stenciled with a frieze of a village scene. The trompe l'oeil hooked rug and rag runner (right) look so real that guests often reach down and touch them to quiet their confusion.

Painting walls, floors, fabric, or furniture requires little equipment and is a talent anyone can master. It can be as simple as rolling new color on the walls, or as intricate as marbleizing, which

makes a surface look like it's made of stone. The effect can be striking, whether it's a pounce-painted floor, a sponge-painted flea-market shelf, an old hope chest feather-painted to look like burled wood, or the inside of a cupboard coated in a surprise color such as watermelon. Paint can transform a tray or update a lamp base. Underfoot, a painted floor or a canvas floorcloth can substitute for a rug. A wooden screen made of hinged plywood panels, painted on both sides, can turn one room into two. The possibilities are endless.

In the early days of our country, whitewash was a quick way to brighten up a space. But color also abounded. Rich saturated tones decorated the walls in many a home, although the evidence was often lost under layers of wallpaper as a family's fortunes improved. Paint also performed marvelous masquerades. With the help of feathers, sea sponges, and bunched-up rags, plain surfaces were made to look like fancier materials, and tricked the eye into seeing ordinary furniture and woodwork made of humble materials such as pine and birch as something much grander. Faux finishes imitated the elaborate grains of fashionable inlaid and imported woods (faux bois) or expensive marble (faux marbre) that were beyond the means of ordinary citizens. At George Washington's estate in Mount Vernon, Virginia, wood was painted and coated with sand to look like limestone.

These age-old hand painting techniques are easily mastered and are an imaginative way to give your surroundings new style and panache. Special brushes make the job surprisingly easy. A brush called a sword liner creates marble veins when it is swirled, rubber rockers similar to rubber stamps transfer their wood-grain pattern to any surface, and fan brushes impart the same effect. A triangular rubber patterning comb is expressly made to create wood grains or stylized squiggles. Find these detailing supplies at art stores and paint shops,

Many countries use color as an antidote to long, cold winters. Norwegian rosemaling, German tole painting, Ukranian folk painting, and traditional Swedish folk motifs inspire spirited designs like those that embellish these painted door panels (opposite). The designs may be sketched beforehand, but they are usually painted freehand in a symmetrical fashion.

along with craft-size bottles of historic paint colors. A paint color on a chart or paint chip will appear darker when used on large areas (such as the walls of a room), so choose a shade several times lighter than the chip.

To give a piece of furniture an aged look, distress the surface after you paint using sandpaper and steel wool, or a hammer and brick. For streaky, Old World walls—the kind you might find in a country villa—spread several similar colors of glaze over a wall, then swirl the colors slightly using a cheesecloth and allow them to dry. For a crackled finish that looks genuinely aged, brush watered-down white glue over a dry, painted surface, then apply a coat of paint on top right away. The paint will crackle as it dries, and your piece will look as though it's been sitting in a barn for years. Painting with a sponge, or sponging, mimics the clayware of

Decorative stenciling enhances window treatments—or substitutes for them. Swaglike floral stencilwork takes the place of curtains around the window of a bedroom-turned-bathroom (opposite). The beadboard walls and the use of several different colors make this window treatment time-consuming but very rewarding. In a bedroom (above), a simple repeat stencil in one color gives the canvas shades a custom look.

One piece of painted furniture can set the style for an entire room. The fanciful place settings painted on the table (above) look like giant plates of fruit, and suggest the work of Peter Hunt, an American artist who painted from the 1940s through the 1960s and was known for his blithesome designs executed with fat, curving brush strokes.

The miniature trunk embellished with Pennsylvania Dutch-style motifs (opposite) is backed by a small, carved statue with a similar patriotic bent.

earlier centuries. Use a natural sea sponge or a synthetic sponge with an open texture so the new finish has gaps and irregularities. Ragging a surface with a bunched-up cloth or stippling it with a stippling brush creates other unique effects. To see where touch-ups or more detailing are necessary, do as artists do: Check your design in a mirror. This reveals gaps more easily than with the eye alone.

To practice decorative painting on a small scale, start with a mirror frame, picture frame, Christmas ornament, metal or wood box, the woodwork in a small room, or the panels on the back of a door. These one-day projects aren't daunting, the results are fast, and the techniques can easily be repeated on a larger scale. Before stenciling an entire dining room floor, for instance, use the floor of a small entrance foyer as a proving ground. Stenciling has a friendly air, and its folksy,

Capture the warmth and patina of a country antique, even if your piece isn't as old as the antique jelly cupboard (opposite). Applying and rubbing off paint, sanding along the edges, and using traditional hues and products such as milk paint will give furniture an authentic look.

A coat of paint in a country blue color makes the reproduction hanging shelf (above) look almost as old as the lovely antique table beneath it.

warm look cheers any surface. Fabric or wallpaper can inspire a stencil design that is repeated all over the walls of a room like wallpaper, or reined in to form a delicate border or frieze at the top of a wall or above the baseboards. When a window frames a beautiful view, stenciling can stand in for curtains. This technique is especially effective in bathrooms and bedrooms, where it amplifies the intimate ambience. Roll-up window shades, Roman shades, and white or ivory curtains and valances are also ready canvases for stenciling with fabric paint or stamping with a combination of large-scale rubber stamps and permanent ink.

Stencil patterns sometimes imitate the colorful, free-spirited strokes and symbols of tole painting, a style of folk painting used by generations of artists in New England, Pennsylvania, and Connecticut to decorate tin; *tôle* means "tin" in French. A stencil design can be transferred to a piece of Mylar or oiled stencil paper and cut out with a craft knife, while a graphic pattern like a checkerboard is best mapped out with masking tape directly onto the surface being stenciled.

Itinerant Colonial stencilers were known for their straightforward, rather flat-effect paintings, while so-called European stenciling is softer and more shaded. Instead of pouncing on the pattern with a round brush, a flat white-bristled half-inch brush is used. The paint is gently dabbed on in a circular motion with the almost-dry brush. Working from the outside of the stencil in, shading is built up while the paint is still wet, leaving a lighter area in the middle for shape and dimension. A scrap of velour fabric can substitute for a stenciling brush, but then shading is less subtle.

Stairways are the perfect place to experiment with stenciling. The inherent structure of steps and risers, banisters and balusters, sets up a built-in repeat pattern, and copying a simple design over and over guarantees a strong result.

A classic country checkerboard adds freshness wherever it appears. To create the simple checkerboard frieze (opposite) that coordinates with the gingham-covered window seat, paint a band of white around the room, then cut a household sponge into a square. Dip it in pink paint, blot off the excess paint on a paper towel or rag, then stamp each square with one press of the sponge. Wicker chairs are easy to spray-paint and take wonderfully to bright colors. Choose a dry, still day to paint and work outside on drop cloths or newspapers.

Long ago, Colonial stencils imitated
expensive wallpapers and painted murals;
today, the stenciling itself is prized. The
bedroom (left and above) is festooned with
designs first discovered in the eighteenth-
century home of a New Hampshire sea
captain. The jewel-like stencils by artist
Adele Bishop are generously spaced on
freshly painted white walls; the slight sheen
of an eggshell finish makes it easy to wipe
away errant smudges and mistakes.

A modest investment in paints and brushes and a few ordinary household items are all that's needed to begin a stenciling project. Traditional stencil designs are very versatile and can be interpreted in a great many ways. The same stencil pattern used in various ways creates different looks in three different houses. This particular pattern was designed by Moses Eaton, Sr., a renowned eighteenth-century stencilist (1753-1833) whose son won a following of his own in carrying on the business. The eye is drawn upward by scarlet and gold stenciling in the dining room of a renovated Maryland home (opposite). The same delicate oak leaf, without the accompanying border, is rendered anew with a single shade of blue in the bedroom of a Colonial house in Maryland (top left). Trios of leaves, widely spaced, give an airy, windswept look to the stenciling in the bedroom (bottom left); the colors are repeated in the window trim and the curtains.

Stenciled floors are colorful, fun, and, unlike a rug, impossible to trip on! A crisp checkerboard design is simple to make; the floor is measured, marked, masked, and then rolled with paint. A painted pattern like diamonds can camouflage traces of wear on an old pine floor, as it does in the entry of a New Hampshire house (opposite).

In the sitting area of a large kitchen in North Carolina, the wide-plank floor's checkerboard pattern was painted with water-based paint and then sealed with several coats of polyurethane. Under the kitchen table, the floor is painted and then stenciled in the same tones to look like a stenciled antique floorcloth.

A delicate trellis stencil combined with freehand vines decorates the light wood floor of a bedroom (overleaf).

Painted Vine Border

The softly flowing vine with its ripe fruit was painted in oil paints that look translucent against the depth of a mottled wall painted in two shades of the same color, here, pale gold and pumpkin. The terra cotta pig adds a note of humor.

MATERIALS

Large sheets of tracing paper

Pencil

Graphite paper

One tube each of artist's oil paints in brown, red, yellow, green

Turpentine or linseed oil

TOOLS

Artist's small tapered brush

Artist's liner brush

Palette

FINISHED SIZE: AS PICTURED, 46" LONG

ACTUAL-SIZE PATTERN

PLANNING THE BORDER

Artist Pia Sjölin-Hart penciled her design directly on the wall. If you do not want to draw freehand on the wall, sketch on large sheets of tracing paper taped together to the length and height of the space. With a pencil mark a center dot that corresponds to the one in the diagram below. Referring to the diagram and using the actual-size pattern, draw three leaves forming a 5-inch equilateral triangle. Draw stems that meet at the dot. From the center dot, draw a gently curving line out to the right, for the vine. Draw the mirror image of the vine out to the left. Continue to draw elements on one side, then repeat them on the other, following the diagram. For the fruit, draw 2- to 3-inch circles. Tape up the finished sketch and view it from across the room. Make any adjustments. Then place graphite paper between the sketch and the wall, and go over design with pencil to transfer it to the wall.

PAINTING THE VINE

Paint the vine first, using the liner brush and brown paint thinned with turpentine or linseed oil. Paint each leaf using the small tapered brush and green paint lightened and thinned. While the paint is still wet, use the liner brush and unthinned green paint to outline the leaf and add veins. Lastly, paint the fruit, thinning the red paint at the center for a dimensional, translucent effect. Allow the paint to dry overnight.

A Wall of Stenciled Stars

MATERIALS

Milk paint in dark blue and orange

Pencil

¼ yard clear, self-adhesive vinyl

TOOLS

Large foam brushes for painting walls

Scissors

Foam stencil brush, or 4-inch squares of cotton velveteen or flannel fabric

Newspaper or paper towels

FINISHED SIZE: MOTIFS ARE 1" AND 1½" IN DIAMETER

ACTUAL-SIZE PATTERN

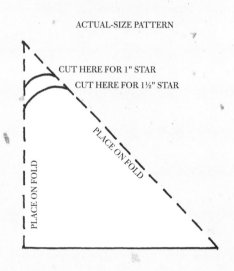

CUT HERE FOR 1" STAR
CUT HERE FOR 1½" STAR

PLACE ON FOLD

PLACE ON FOLD

Little stars, created from a cut-and-fold stencil much like a snowflake made in childhood, stand out in orange against a wall of dark blue. Milk paint with its warm, old-time texture was used for both the wall and the stars.

PAINTING THE BACKGROUND

Following the manufacturer's instructions, mix the blue milk paint powder with water to obtain a creamy consistency. Use a foam brush to paint at least two coats, letting the paint dry after each coat.

CUTTING THE STENCILS

Trace or photocopy the actual-size pattern. Cut out along dash and straight lines and remove the smaller wedge at the center. Cut clear self-adhesive vinyl into 4-inch squares. Fold one in half vertically, horizontally, and then diagonally so it is folded in eighths. Place the pattern on top. For the 1-inch star, trace the small curved line between fold

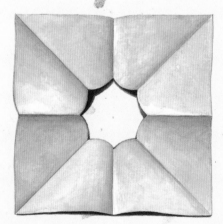

lines, cut it out, and unfold the stencil. Repeat to make several more small stencils. Then cut the deeper curved line on the pattern and repeat the process to make several stencils for the larger 1½-inch star.

STENCILING

Peel off the paper backing from the self-adhesive vinyl stencils, and press them onto the wall in a random pattern. Work on one area at a time.

Mix the orange milk paint powder with very little water to make a paste-like consistency. For an applicator, use a foam stencil brush or wrap a square of fabric around your index finger. Dip the applicator into the paint; then remove the excess paint evenly by pouncing on a paper towel or newspaper. Press the edges of a stencil tightly to the wall with your thumb. With the applicator fairly dry of paint, apply the paint in an up-and-down motion, starting at the edges of the cutout and working in toward the center. Repeat with each stencil.

Leave the stencils on the wall until the paint is at least somewhat dry, then lift off the stencils and reapply them in another area. The stencils can be reused a few times.

A Stenciled
Leaf Frieze

Two repeats of a stencil motif that dates back to Colonial times top off a shelf full of antique collectibles. To add complexity, a geometric design created with purchased, pre-cut stencils frames the entire piece.

MATERIALS

2 large sheets of clear acetate or mylar

Pre-cut geometric stencils

Pencil

Crayon

Permanent black fine-point felt-tip marker

Spray adhesive or rubber cement

Japan paints or acrylic paints in red and blue-gray

TOOLS

Scissors

Craft knife #1 or artist's matte knife

Cutting mat

Scraps of cotton velour fabric or 2 stencil brushes

Palette

FINISHED SIZE: ONE REPEAT IS 4¾" HIGH BY 13¼" LONG

PREPARING THE WALLS

Before you begin, make sure the walls are clean and dry. If you give the walls a fresh coat of paint, use paint in a semigloss or eggshell finish so any small mistakes in stenciling can be wiped off easily. Save some of the wall paint for touch-ups later.

CHOOSING A METHOD

You can emulate the authentic stencil process used in Colonial times, one that results in a softer, subtler texture, by using quick-drying japan paints and a 4-inch square of velour fabric wrapped around your index finger for an applicator. For easier application and cleanup, washable acrylic paints and stencil brushes—bristle or foam—are a good choice.

DETERMINING THE LAYOUT

Keeping in mind the symmetry of the design and the length of a full repeat of three leaves, plan the position of the stencils. Allow at least ½ inch and preferably 1 to 2 inches between full repeats, but this spacing may be adjusted as necessary. If you like, center photocopies of the design over an architectural focal point such as a window, door, or

mantel, or piece of furniture such as a wall shelf. Or repeat just one leaf to fill a small area. Avoid working around a corner.

When you know where you want to place the design, make light marks on the wall with a pencil. Trim the acetate sheets with scissors so that they fit the space between the door or window molding and the ceiling or ceiling molding. Position the photocopies in this space, and then mark guidelines on the acetate in crayon.

MAKING THE STENCILS

Trace the actual-size patterns on pages 104 and 105 for the leaves and include the large plus (+) signs, the registration marks. These signs will help you align the acetate sheets to cut a stencil for each color. To trace the design, place one sheet of acetate over the pattern. Using a felt-tip marker, trace the large and small leaves and the plus signs. Make a second tracing identical to the first on the other sheet of acetate. Trim the acetate sheets, leaving a 1-inch margin around the design.

Working on a cutting mat or protected surface, cut out those areas shown on the patterns in blue-gray on one piece of acetate for stencil #1, and those areas shown in red

on the other sheet of acetate for stencil #2. Use a craft knife with a fresh blade; replace the blade if it tears rather than cuts cleanly. Always cut toward you, rotating the acetate as necessary to cut the curved lines.

STENCILING THE FIRST COLOR

If you like, practice stenciling on piece of posterboard before you stencil on the wall. Spray the back of the acetate with adhesive, or apply rubber cement. Let either adhesive dry for a few minutes until it is tacky to the touch so it will provide a temporary bond.

Press stencil #1 in place. Press the edges of each cutout area tightly to the surface. Pour blue-gray paint onto the palette. Dip the applicator, either velour fabric wrapped around your finger or a brush, into the paint, and pounce off the excess onto newspaper so the applicator is nearly dry. Dab lightly onto the cutout areas of the stencil, beginning at the edges and working inward. Use an up-and-down motion rather than straight or circular strokes. Let the paint dry slightly (a hair dryer will speed this process). Lift stencil #1 straight up and reposition it 1 inch away or a distance previously determined. Complete stenciling with stencil #1 and remove the stencil after the paint has dried slightly.

STENCILING THE SECOND COLOR

Apply stencil #2, aligning it so the cutout areas lie within the previously stenciled areas. Using the same technique of pouncing up and down, stencil the inside areas of the leaves with red paint. Let the paint dry slightly. Lift the stencil straight up and reposition it for the second repeat. Remove the stencil after the paint has dried slightly; then let the design dry completely.

Stenciling Tips

◆ Invest in a cutting mat and a good craft knife and learn to use them safely.

◆ Tape and re-cut any mistakes that occur in cutting the stencils because they will be glaringly apparent when the stencil has been painted on the wall.

◆ If the design is simple, cut several copies so you can continue the repeat without waiting for the paint to dry.

◆ Cut the top of the stencil even with the ceiling molding or window molding so you won't have to measure the placement of the stencil each time, as you move around the room.

◆ To avoid cutting stencils altogether, take a look at the plethora of pre-cut stencils on the market, combine several of them for an authenic historical look.

◆ Always stand back from your work to judge the overall effect.

A Faux
~ Scatter Rug ~

Whimsically casual and a bit witty rather than trompe l'oeil,

as it doesn't really fool the eye, this rug was painted

directly on the floor of an entry area.

The outline of the rug was marked and the floor

all around it was given a coat of blue milk paint

before the runner was painted.

MATERIALS

Milk paint in blue, dark green, off-white, black, cream, marigold yellow, pumpkin, and barn red

TOOLS

Pencil

Yardstick

T square

Newspaper

Masking tape

Long-handled paint roller

Artist's brushes: tapered, flat, and liner

FINISHED SIZE: 17" BY 33"

MAKING THE PAINT

To make the milk paint, follow the manufacturer's instructions on mixing the milk paint powder with water to obtain a creamy consistency. Mix the powders to produce the colors indicated in the directions.

PAINTING THE FLOOR

To recreate Michal Mitchell Small's design, begin with a clean floor. With a pencil, yardstick, and T square, mark a 17-by-33-inch rectangle on the floor for the rug. To mask the entire rectangle, place newspaper in the rectangle and secure it with masking tape, keeping the tape inside the marked lines. Paint the floor with a mixture of blue and a little dark green. Do not paint in the taped rectangle. Use a long-handled roller and leave streaks, or let the paint dry and rub the floor with sandpaper to distress the surface. Save a small amount of the floor color paint to paint around the fringed tassels later. When the paint is dry, remove the newspaper.

PAINTING THE RUG BACKGROUND

Following the diagram on page 108, use a pencil and yardstick to mark the areas for the fringe and the pumpkin-colored border. To paint the rug background, tape the border area by placing tape inside the center rectangle and outside the outline of the entire rug. Paint the border with pumpkin, mixed with a little barn red. Allow the paint to dry and remove the tape. To paint the center rectangle, place tape outside the marked edge. Paint the area with cream mixed with a little marigold yellow. Allow the paint to dry and remove the tape.

MARKING THE DESIGN

Trace or photocopy the actual-size patterns on page 109. Place several sheets of paper together under the patterns so you can cut out the necessary number of patterns for each shape. You will need 1 fringe shape, 4 grape clusters, 4 fleurs-de-lis, and 10 leaves.

Place the fringe at the end of the two shorter sides of the rug and trace around the shape, repeating it all the way across. Arrange the remaining templates on the cream center of the rug, referring to the diagram for their placement. Trace around each shape, then connect the leaves with two curving vines drawn freehand as shown. Add tendrils along the vines.

PAINTING THE MOTIFS

Use a small tapered brush to paint all the shapes, shading all but the fringe with a little off-white. Paint the fleurs-de-lis blue, the leaves dark green, and the grapes purple, a mixture of blue and barn red.

To paint the fringe, use marigold yellow mixed with a little pumpkin. Allow the paint to dry. Use a liner brush to paint black strands on the fringe. Use a small, flat brush to paint a black line inside the center rectangle and to draw the connecting vines with pumpkin paint.

Add black to each color mixed for the shapes and outline each shape. Also with the darker shade and with the small, flat brush, add circular definition to the grapes, draw veins on the leaves, and add tendrils. Use the floor color to paint in between the tassels of the fringe.

When the paint is thoroughly dry, apply at least two coats of varnish or polyurethane to the floor.

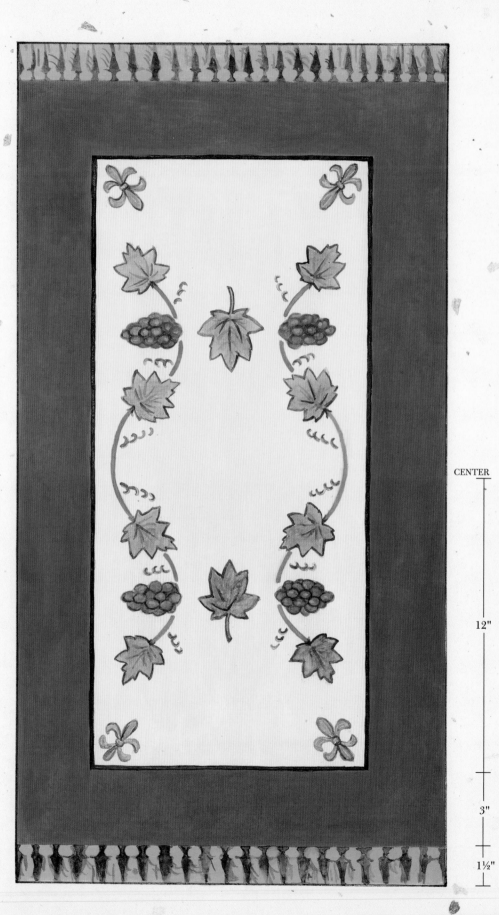

CENTER

12"

3"

1½"

Patterns for the Scatter Rug

FLEUR-DE-LIS

TENDRILS

GRAPE CLUSTER

LEAF

FRINGE

ACTUAL-SIZE PATTERNS

A Diamond Checkerboard Floorcloth

Floorcloths can be made in any size—from a huge square that covers a living room floor to a small rectangular doormat. Painted in colors and designs to match your decor, floorcloths are convenient because they can be sponge-mopped clean and rolled up for storage.

PREPARING THE CANVAS

Measure the area you want the rug to cover, add 2 inches to each dimension, and cut the canvas to this size. If the canvas is not wide enough to accommodate the size you need, piece it: Cut two panels and place them together with right (or gessoed) sides facing. Machine-sew along the ungessoed margins, or 1 inch from the selvage edges. On the wrong side, apply rubber cement to the seam allowances, allow it to dry for a few minutes until it is tacky to the touch, then use a brayer or rolling pin to press the seam allowances open and flat against the back of the floorcloth.

For smaller floorcloths, you can use 3- or 6-yard rolls of pre-gessoed canvas. It comes in 52-inch (standard width), 72-inch, or 84-inch widths.

Unless the canvas has come gessoed, use a paint roller to apply one coat of gesso over the entire right side of floorcloth and let the gesso dry completely.

Using a paint roller, apply two coats of latex paint in the background color to the canvas, letting each coat dry.

MARKING THE DIAMOND CHECKERBOARD

Locate the center of the floorcloth. Use a yardstick and a pencil to lightly mark lines from the center out to each corner, making a big X. Mark off 6-inch increments along each arm of the X, stopping after the same number of increments for a square, and at least 12 inches from the corners of the canvas for any square or rectangle (a, page 112). Connect the outermost marks on each leg of the X to form a large square or rectangle. Extend lines from the marks, parallel to the legs of the X, out to this large rectangle. This will create a checkerboard with squares on the diagonal. For the inner border, use a yardstick and a pencil to draw lines 1 inch beyond the large rectangle, and for the outer border, a line 6 inches beyond that (b, page 113). The middle border is between these lines.

MASKING OFF THE AREAS

To mask off the middle border, place masking tape on the inside of the outer border all around the rug; use a craft knife or razor blade to cut the tape cleanly to make sharply

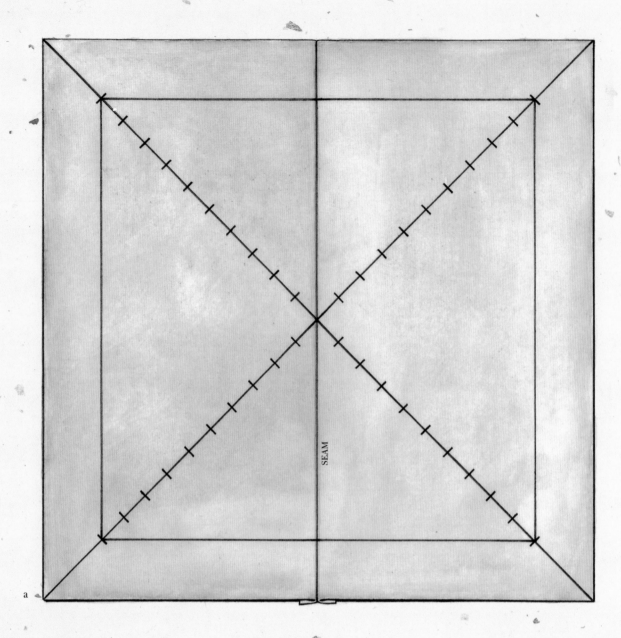

SEAM

a

masked corners. Then place tape on the outside of the inner border. In between these pieces of tape, tape strips of brown paper.

If you do not have a 6-inch quilter's square, make a template: Use a pencil and a T square to mark a 6-inch square on cardboard and cut it out. Using the template and brown paper, cut out half the number of squares marked on the canvas. Cut out about 10 extra brown paper squares and cut them in half diagonally to mask the triangles along the edges of the design. Brush the

edges of the squares and triangles with rubber cement, or spray them with adhesive; let them dry for a few minutes until they are tacky to the touch, for a temporary bond. Press the brown paper squares over every other marked square of the checkerboard. Press the brown paper triangles over the triangles at the edge of the design to continue the checkerboard all the way to the border.

To ensure crisp edges on the design, spray the entire surface with a light coat of clear acrylic spray, or apply matte gel

medium with a roller. This seals all the edges and prevents paint from seeping underneath the paper or masking tape.

PAINTING THE CONTRASTING COLOR

Place newspaper under the edges of the canvas all around the rug. Use a roller to apply the contrasting color paint to the unmasked areas. Make sure you apply the paint all the way to the edge on all sides. Apply two coats of paint, letting each coat dry.

6"

1"

6"

b

FINISHING

When the paint is completely dry, remove the masking tape and all the brown paper. If the surface was sealed before the contrasting color was rolled on, there should be little or no paint seepage. If any edges are fuzzy or the paint has run, use artist's brushes and the background color to touch up these areas. Erase any visible pencil marks.

Turn the floorcloth over to the back, and brush rubber cement 1 inch from the edge on all four sides. Let the rubber cement dry slightly until it is tacky to the touch, then fold the edges over. Cut the excess canvas at the corners diagonally to reduce bulk (c). Use a rolling pin to press the edges flat. Secure the edges with masking tape or spring-clamp clothespins to hold the folded edge until the rubber cement bonds.

Apply two light coats of a varnish sealer, more for a floorcloth that will have to withstand a lot of foot traffic. Use a roller or foam brush to apply the varnish and allow each coat to dry thoroughly.

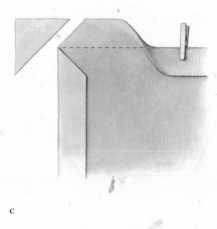

c

Leaf Printed Curtains

This decorative window treatment invites the outdoors in. Created by an interior designer and decorative painter for her own home, the curtains were stamped with leaves from the trees right outside the window. This easy technique will work on walls, tablecloths and napkins, and even clothing.

PREPARING THE FABRIC

If you are making the curtains, before you begin, wash the fabric to pre-shrink it and to remove sizing. Cut out the fabric for the panels and valance but do not sew them.

STAMPING THE DESIGN

To recreate Pia Sjölin-Hart's design, protect the work surface with a plastic dropcloth. Mix the paints to create new shades, if you like, adding a little water for a creamy consistency. Using a fresh sheet of newspaper each time, paint one side of a leaf, brushing in the direction of the veins. Place the leaf on the fabric and press on it, smoothing the stem as well, then lift the leaf straight up. If the paint is too watery, the color will run. If the paint is too thick, the veins and texture will not show up. Adjust the paint mixture, if necessary. For a more translucent print, press a leaf onto the fabric twice without rebrushing it. To avoid smudges, clean your hands with a rag before working on the next leaf.

For the curtain panels, use a large leaf, such as a hickory leaf, turned in different directions or a grouping of several leaves on a stem. Stamp beyond the raw edges, so the design is not bound by hard edges. Vary the intensity of the prints; an occasional heavy or weak print is part of the charm of the design. Use one color at a time, starting with the darker one. When you have stamped all the leaves in olive, let the paint dry. Then stamp with moss green, overlapping the olive leaves. Let the paint dry. To add liveliness and to camouflage any smudges, spritz yellow paint over the leaf prints. Dip a toothbrush into the yellow paint and run your finger over the bristles, spraying dots of paint onto the fabric.

For the valance, use long leaves in varying sizes, such as an American chestnut, but keep the tips of the largest leaves 2 inches from the bottom edge.

FINISHING

Heat-set the fabric following the paint manufacturer's instructions, either by tumbling the fabric in a dryer, or by ironing over the paint with a dry press cloth.

for love of
FABRIC

S titchery has a lure all its own, and speaks to those who appreciate its pleasures: a patchwork pattern emerging from squares of cloth arranged just so; the rainbow of a thread display; sharpened needles at the ready in a tomato pincushion.

Quilts can be as striking as paintings. The stark simplicity of a patchwork quilt design called Squares in Squares gives an entrance hall a sophisticated air (opposite). A doll in Amish clothing rests in the window of an Ohio farmhouse (right). Amish dolls have no faces. Humility is an important Amish precept; creating a likeness is believed to raise oneself above God.

In the 1800s, stitchery was a necessity, not a choice; all women were required to sew. It was customary for a woman's dowry to include handmade quilts, important household items as essential as food in keeping a family alive. Making quilts was

part of a young girl's preparation for life. The quilt tops were usually stitched long before she had met her mate. Then, when an engagement was set, the tops were stitched to batting and backing to make a dozen finished quilts, and then a thirteenth was added, an all-white wedding quilt, or "bride's quilt," the finest one in the dowry. Some brides preferred to sew the wedding quilt entirely by themselves. Others shared the task with friends at a quilting bee, one of the liveliest forms of entertainment and information-gathering in the early days of our country, needles flying over the snowy cloth as conversation flowed around the room.

Friendship quilts were made by a group of people, with each block stitched and signed by a different hand. Friendship quilts served as a reminder of precious ties and were presented by a group, as a remembrance of a special occasion or to celebrate the life of someone who was leaving the community, such as a young bride and her new husband heading out West, or someone who had performed a good work, such as a favorite teacher or a revered minister.

Scrap fabric not fine enough for quilts was ideal for rug making. Most houses had some kind of floor covering by the 1830s, often tacked down over cedar sprigs for a fresh scent or over straw sprinkled with tobacco and black pepper to combat moths. Carpeting imported from Turkey or Persia was too expensive for some families, but smaller rugs were easy to make, and it was customary to have a rug, often a hooked one, on the hearth. To make a hooked rug, a design is drawn or stenciled on backing fabric such as burlap, feed sacks, or canvas held taut within a frame. Cloth or yarn scraps are then woven through the backing using a specially designed hook some say was adapted from a sailor's tool used to weave these rugs at sea. The earliest hooked rugs were made from worn cotton clothing; today, wool is the fabric of choice because of its durability.

Instead of making these Log Cabin squares into a quilt, groups of two are joined end to end to make a long runner with bound edges for the dining table of a farmhouse in Norway (opposite). Dark patches at intersecting corners form the pattern's distinctive crosslike effect. Like most Log Cabin coverlets, this piece is not quilted. On a pencil-post bed festooned with rose-hip vines (overleaf) is a colorful 1910 quilt. A hooked rug lies at bedside, warming the sisal rug, while yo-yo pillows on the bed lend a whimsical note.

Stripes, checks, plaids, and tweeds add texture and interest, especially when hooked in curving lines that give the impression of dimension. To achieve a soft and varied effect, fabrics can be toned down or muted by dyeing over the original color with shades such as khaki, black, and olive green.

Making hooked rugs was a popular handcraft in Colonial America, and today's revival of interest speaks to its allure, and to the rugs' endearing depictions of simple things both personal and charming. Houses, flowers, and pets are favorite subjects of the so-called primitive-style hooked rug, which shows a naive pattern made with wide strips of fabric. Narrower strips of wool or yarn and more sophisticated designs characterize the traditional, or realistic, hooked rug. To preserve a hooked rug and show off its design, it can be displayed as a wall

A colorful quilt can make even the simplest room come alive. The vibrant pattern of an early-nineteenth-century Star quilt (opposite) takes center stage in a neutral colored room. The bowtie design on the bed (above), Courthouse Steps, is a variation of the Log Cabin pattern. Repeating large blocks of color gives the quilt a contemporary look.

Pastel colors and a Sunbonnet Sue motif identify the quilt (top right) as dating from 1930, when this quilt pattern and soft-toned fabrics were all the rage. Delicately stenciled walls translate the hues and motifs of an 1830 Flower Basket quilt (bottom right), one variation of the ever-popular Basket pattern. The Japanese Pavilion at the 1876 Centennial Exposition in Philadelphia inspired renewed interest in Asian design, and the Fan became a popular design theme through the 1920s and 1930s. The Fan pattern was also popular with Amish quilters, who were drawn to its simplicity. The Fan quilt (opposite) shows off an inspired mix of textured menswear fabrics highlighted by triangular wedges of brilliant red. Fan quilts often include fancy fabrics such as velvet and satin. Embroidery stitches worked over the seams are also typical.

hanging, or strategically placed in an open area or in a lightly traveled corner.

Braided rugs and woven or crocheted rag rugs are faster and easier to make than hooked rugs. They require no drawing or designing, just plentiful fabric scraps. Like hooked rugs, they have always been a fine complement to country furnishings and are easily adapted to many color schemes.

Penny rugs are lightweight rugs made from coin-shaped pieces of felt and wool. Layering fabric circles one on top of the other creates the lively geometric patterns. A penny rug can also be made with oval-shaped pieces or with both circles and ovals. Too fragile to be used on the floor, they are perfect for tabletops.

Samplers are a charming mixture of stitchery, verse, and color, typically made by young girls to show off their handwork. Often sentimental in nature, they are precious examples of perseverence and aptitude. The earliest samplers were portable records of favorite embroidery patterns and motifs made when cloth was more readily available than paper. Embellishing household linens, clothing, and pillows was easy with this reference in hand. A sampler could be rolled up and stored, and was traditionally passed from generation to generation, becoming ever more cherished with time. Samplers are small enough to have survived far longer than many other antiques. Some were made to commemorate an anniversary or the birth of a child; others, called mourning samplers, recalled the dead, and sometimes included human hair. Verses from poetry or the Bible were incorporated into some of the designs, either in the body or the border, and helped a child memorize treasured hymns and prayers.

All these forms of handwork bring history to life. From these documents of cloth, we learn much about the people of the past. Taking up needle and thread at the start of a new century will provide testaments for the future.

Yo-yos are little circles of fabric gathered into small, finished puffs. They combine in a tour-de-force mosaic on the coverlet (opposite). Popular as summer spreads during the 1930s and 1940s, these wonderful coverlets can still be found, though usually in need of a few repair stitches. The design is yet another variation on the traditional American scrap quilt, the festive effect resulting from the great variety of dressweight print fabrics. More than 1,300 yo-yos are needed for a coverlet of this size; the yo-yos can be hand stitched or purchased ready-made.

Hanging a quilt from the ceiling (left) is an idea rooted in history. When houses were too small for quilting frames, the frames were hoisted to the ceiling when not in use, then pulled down for quilting bees. The owners of this wood frame pioneer house in northern Florida found hooks in their living room ceiling; several elderly neighbors remembered the house as the site of frequent quilting bees. So once again, a quilting frame was hung from the ceiling and a quilt laced taut on the frame. The only difference: The quilt is displayed face down so everyone can appreciate its design. On the floor, a crocheted rug mirrors some of its colors.

Every hooked rug has a story to tell. Choosing and planning the design is usually a thoughtful, personal process, which accounts for a hooked rug's charm. The design can be enlarged to a suitable size using a photocopier, then transferred to the burlap background of the rug. From then on, hooking a rug is like a paint-by-numbers technique, though the "painting" is done with strips of wool. The right mix of textures and colors creates rich, dimensional shading, giving a design such as the elegant multimasted sailing ship (opposite) a feeling of life and motion. Solid colors have a flatter effect, as in the playful house design (above left) and the storybook rug from the 1930s (above right), that hangs above a pair of folk carvings that debuted as gateposts a hundred years ago. Surrounding a hooked rug with a dark border gives the effect of a frame, whether the rug is displayed on the wall or covers the floor (overleaf). Designer Claire Murray created the multicolored rugs on the floor as well as the romantic one on the wall for her renovated Colonial farmhouse in western New Hampshire.

In nineteenth-century New England and Quebec, penny rugs were as popular as hooked rugs, but they are less well known today. Some say large copper pennies were used as templates for the earliest penny rugs, hence their name. Made by combining circle- and tongue-shaped fabrics, the rugs are commonly displayed on tables or walls because they are not durable enough to stand much foot traffic. Penny rugs are usually decorated with a blanket stitch, and sometimes the coins and tongues are embroidered or appliquéd as well. Overlapping felt tongues characterize the colorful penny rug used as a table runner (above). The rug is embroidered with double cross-stitch stars. The striking late-nineteenth-century prism-shaped penny rug (opposite) was found at a garage sale and now hangs like a stained-glass window on the wall of an 1899 Ohio schoolhouse converted to a home. On the floor, a rag rug with an interesting swirled design reinterprets the muted color scheme of the vintage penny rug.

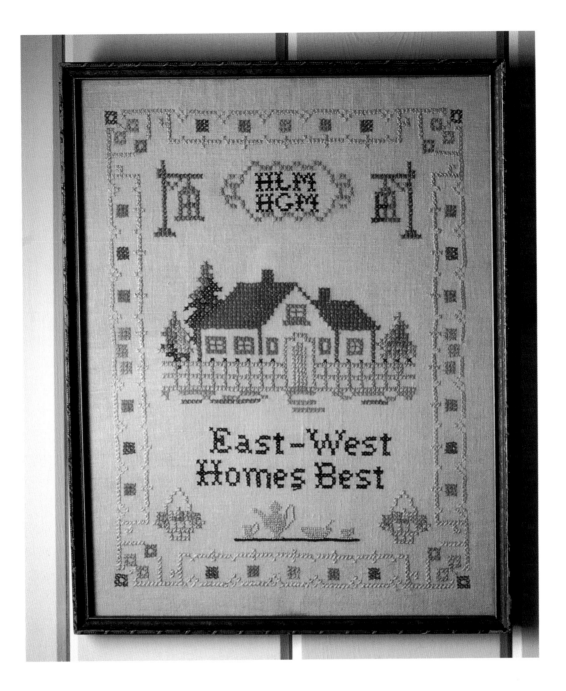

Samplers show off stitching skills, and typically commemorate girls' rites of passage. Motifs include the alphabet, family trees, birds, beasts, and homes. Samplers helped teach lessons in basic needlework, geography, and even multiplication, both at home and at school. In the guest bedroom of an Ohio log home (opposite), samplers created by the homeowner's seven sisters and her 94-year-old aunt hang over the bed as remembrances of family life. The dainty Minnesota sampler stitched in the 1930s or 1940s (above) now makes its home with other vintage pieces in a renovated 1948 cottage in California. The initials HLM and HGM are most likely those of the woman who stitched the sampler and her husband. When a date is incorporated into the design, the sampler becomes more valuable.

Feline fanciers will love the lounging velvet cats and hooked kitten pillows (opposite); dog lovers can substitute their own favorite pets to fill a bench or basket in the same charming way. Red fringe adds a bright outline to the black velvet pillows. The graphic bench cushion is made up of a trio of Log Cabin pillows set side by side. Most of the mousers in the basket (above) are hand-stitched of soft cottons, glossy satins, and plush velours and stuffed with fiberfill. The faces and whiskers are embroidered. Some of the eyes are stitched on while others are made of small amber-colored buttons.

Compass Circles Hooked Rug

Like any pleasing folk art design, the geometric circles in this rug are appealing and colorful. Created with long strips of wool fabric usually cut from old clothes, hooked rugs became popular in the 1820s when burlap, the backing fabric of choice, became widely available.

MATERIALS

30"-by-40"-rectangle of good quality burlap, 12 to13 threads per inch

3½ yards of twill rug tape, 1¼" wide

Tracing paper

Tightly woven wool fabric: 1½ yards for background, small amounts of assorted colors for motifs

Sewing thread to match burlap

TOOLS

Clear quilter's square or ruler

Hard lead pencil

Pins

Scissors

Rotary cutter

Cutting mat

Embroidery hoop or frame

Rug hook with medium hook

Steam iron

Pressing cloth

Sewing needle

FINISHED SIZE: 22" BY 34"

PREPARING THE BACKGROUND

Use a pencil and a clear quilter's square or ruler to mark a 22-by-34-inch rectangle on the burlap. Make sure the corners are true 90-degree angles.

With a sewing machine, make two rows of stitching ¾-inch beyond the edge of the design. Pin, then stitch rug tape around the edge of the design, easing it around the corners (a, page 142). Turn the tape outward and baste it to the burlap.

MARKING THE DESIGN

Trace the actual-size circle motif on page 142 and cut it out. If you like, duplicate it by tracing or photocopying to obtain 38 motifs. Arrange the motifs on the burlap background in 5 loose rows of 7 or 8 motifs, keeping the motifs at least 1 inch from the tape. For a more regimented design, have the same number of motifs in each row and keep the motifs aligned.

When you are pleased with the arrangement, trace around the circles. Then remove them, and use a ruler and a pencil to mark the horizontal and vertical lines across each circle. For an interesting effect, one

cross may be turned at an angle as is the third circle from the left in the bottom row.

CUTTING THE FABRIC STRIPS

Using a rotary cutter, a clear quilter's ruler, and a cutting mat, cut the fabric into ⅛-inch-wide strips, cutting along the grain. Work with only one layer of fabric at a time so you can cut the longest strips possible.

HOOKING

Place the burlap in a frame or hoop to hold it taut. Hold the hook in your right hand above the burlap and a strip of wool in your left hand beneath the burlap (b, page 142). Push the hook through the burlap, sliding the small shank of the hook between the thumb and finger of your left hand, until it catches the wool strip held between your thumb and forefinger. Pull up the end of the strip, bringing it through to the top; leave it 1 inch high. Put the hook into the next mesh and pull up a loop about ¼ inch. As you pull up each succeeding loop, press the hook against the burlap to make the hole bigger so the hook can pass through with more ease. Keep pulling up the loops evenly, all about ¼

inch high. Skip a mesh occasionally to keep the loops from being packed too tightly; the loops should be close enough to stay in place but not so tight that the rug will buckle. At the end of a strip, bring the end through to the top. Trim this and all the ends later to the same height as the loops.

WORKING THE DESIGN

Begin the design by hooking the circle motifs. Work the outline of the circle and the cross first in one color. For some motifs, use a second color to hook a line on either side of the cross and inside the circular outline. Then fill in each quadrant with another color, carrying the strips under the lines of the cross when going from one quadrant to the next one. Next, work a thin border consisting of three rows around the edge of the burlap rectangle. You can echo the colors used in the crosses on these continuous border lines or use one color throughout if you prefer. Lastly, use one color wool to work the background of the design, filling in between and around the motifs up to the border lines.

FINISHING

Using a damp pressing cloth, steam press the rug thoroughly on the wrong side and again, lightly, on the right side. Trim the excess burlap to 1 inch beyond the two rows of stitching. Pin, then hand-sew the tape to the wrong side of the rug, mitering the corners as you stitch the hem.

Not all rugs are meant to be walked on. Some rugs, antique ones as well as newly made ones, can be hung on the wall like artwork. To hang a hooked rug, a penny rug, a latch hook rug, a quilt, a tapestry, or any large size fiber art, you want to put as little stress as possible on the rug by hanging it to distribute its weight evenly. You can use either one of the two methods described on the facing page.

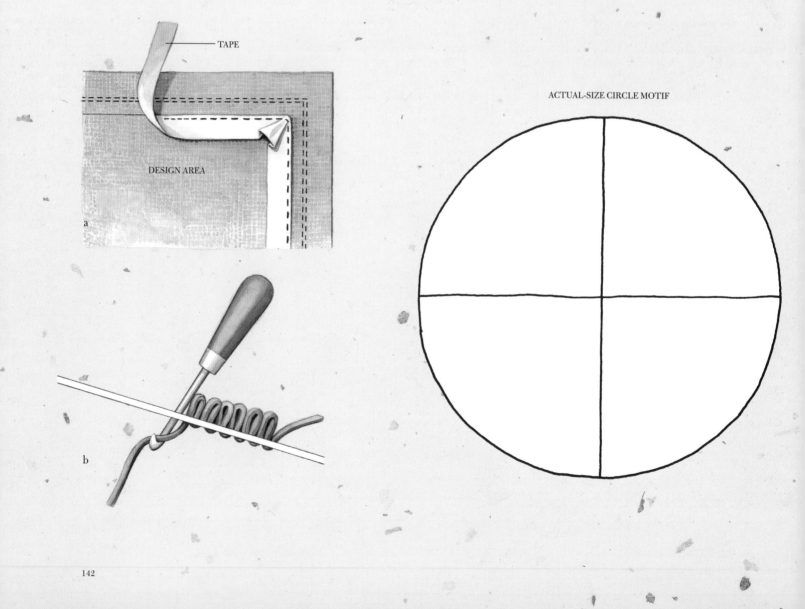

TAPE

DESIGN AREA

a

b

ACTUAL-SIZE CIRCLE MOTIF

Displaying a Hooked Rug

MAKING A CASING

To make a casing you will need a 2-inch-wide (or wider) ribbon or tightly woven fabric with hemmed edges that is 1 inch shorter than the width of the top edge of the rug. Sew the ribbon across the wrong side of the rug near the top edge (a), leaving the two short ends open. Cut a wooden dowel, a wooden slat, or a metal rod ¼ inch shorter than the rug and insert it through the casing, with an equal amount extending from either side. To hang the rug, balance the extended ends of the dowel on screws or nails that have been hammered into the wall.

USING ARTIST'S STRETCHERS

To mount the rug, use artist's stretchers the same size as the rug.

Sew the rug to the center of a sturdy backing fabric such as a medium weight tightly woven cotton or linen fabric cut 4 inches larger all around than the stretcher frame dimensions. Place the backing fabric wrong side up on a work surface and center the stretcher frame on top of it. Use a staple gun and ¼-inch slanted end staples to secure the backing fabric to the wrong side of the stretcher. Start at the midpoints of opposite sides as you pull the backing fabric taut without distorting the grain of the fabric or the rug sewn to it (b). Staple out to the corners. Make neat corners by folding down the top fabric first (c), then bringing the side fabric over on top of it (d).

To hang the rug, insert eyehooks at the sides about one-third of the way down from the top corners (e), stretch picture wire across the back of the frame, and twist the wire ends to secure them.

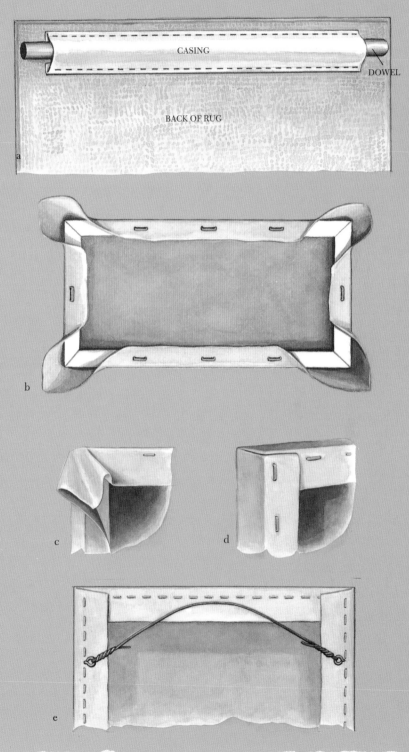

143

~ Penny Rug ~

Named for the coin used as a template, penny rugs are an early New England craft that, like scrap quilts, promoted the use and reuse of fabric scraps. A folk-art mosaic created with circles of wool appliquéd with blanket stitches makes a table covering perfect for traditional or contemporary rooms.

MATERIALS

4 yards of 45"-wide closely woven natural cotton or linen fabric

Medium weight wool fabric (any type including knits), 45"-wide (yardages allow for the shrinkage of felting), or wool felt, 36" wide: 1½ yards each brown and tan, ½ yard each cream and maroon

Extra-strong cotton thread in brown

TOOLS

Brown wrapping paper

Scissors

Pencil

Yardstick

Compass or tracing paper

Glue stick

Cardboard

Permanent fine felt-tip marker

Sewing and embroidery needles

Steam iron

FINISHED SIZE: 36" BY 68"

PREPARING THE BACKGROUND

For the background and the rug backing, make a paper pattern for a diamond shape as follows: Cut a 36-by-68-inch rectangle from a large sheet of brown wrapping paper. Fold the rectangle in half lengthwise and then in half crosswise. Crease the folds, then open the rectangle. Use a pencil and a yardstick to connect the midpoints of each side, as indicated by the folds, to form a diamond. Cut out this diamond shape.

To cut out the rug background, place the diamond pattern on the cotton or linen fabric at least ½ inch from the edges of the fabric and with the folds of the paper along the grain of the fabric. Use a pencil and a yardstick to carefully trace around the diamond; this marks the sewing line or finished surface area of the rug.

To allow for seam allowances, cut out the fabric ½ inch larger than the pattern all around. Cut out a second, identical fabric diamond shape for the rug backing. Set the rug backing aside.

MAKING THE TEMPLATES

To make templates for the design you will need three circles (the "pennies" of long ago), one 1½ inches in diameter, one 2 inches in diameter, and one 2½ inches in diameter. You can make the three circles on paper with a compass or trace the circular patterns on page 147; cut out each circle separately. Glue the circles to sturdy cardboard; let the glue dry, then cut them out.

"FELTING" THE FABRIC

Felting is a process that changes the texture and density of wool fabric, unleashing and intertwining all the fibers in the yarns, and in so doing creates a different, denser fabric which will not unravel when cut. Felted wool is the perfect fabric for a penny rug because the cut edges will not unravel. To felt wool fabrics, wash them in a washing machine with little or no soap; use hot water and regular agitation. Dry the fabrics in a dryer with heat. The fabrics will shrink considerably. Steam press them to smooth them out.

CUTTING THE CIRCLES

Use the templates and a marker to trace and cut out the following: from brown wool, 160 large circles and 160 small circles; from tan wool, 116 medium circles; from cream wool, 80 medium circles; from maroon wool, 36 large circles and 36 small circles.

APPLIQUÉING THE CIRCLES

To form a bull's-eye, center a small circle on a medium circle and center the medium circle on a large circle using the colors indicated below. Use the blanket stitch to secure the small to the medium, and the medium to the large circle, keeping the legs and tops of each stitch about ¼ inch long. In this way, make 80 B bull's-eyes with a large brown, a medium tan, and a small brown. Make 80 C bull's-eyes with a large brown, a medium cream, and a small brown. Make 36 M bull's-eyes with a large maroon, a medium tan, and a small maroon.

ARRANGING THE BULL'S-EYES

On the rug, there are 7 concentric diamonds of bull's-eyes around a center of 4 bull's-eyes. Refer to the diagram, and begin laying out B bull's-eyes all around the diamond, ½ inch from the edge. The edges of the bull's-eyes should just meet; there are 14 of them from each acute angle to each obtuse angle. Arrange a row of C bull's-eyes all around, inside the Bs; stagger their placement so each fits in between two on the outermost row, and all keep the overall diamond shape. Working toward the center, arrange a row of M bull's-eyes, then another row of Bs, then two rows of Cs. Fill in the center with four more Cs. All the motifs should touch and be in straight rows, each row with two more bull's-eyes than the row before. When the arrangement is aligned, pin each bull's-eye in place. Work blanket stitches around the edges of each large circle to secure it.

KEY

B ● = ◉

C ● = ◉

M ● = ◉

FINISHING

With right sides facing, pin the rug background to the backing. Machine or hand-stitch around three sides and around all four corners, ½ inch from edge and leaving a 7-inch opening. Trim the seam allowance at each corner diagonally, and turn rug right side out. Fold the open edges ½ inch to the inside, and slip-stitch the opening closed. Press the rug with a steam iron.

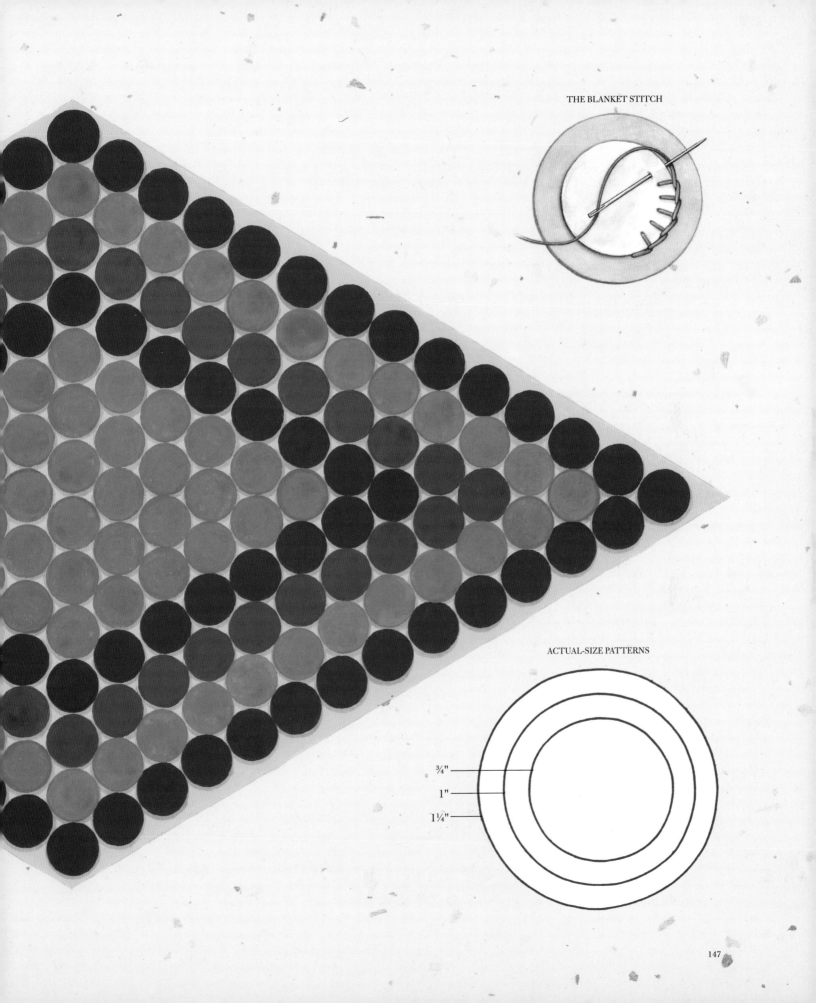

THE BLANKET STITCH

ACTUAL-SIZE PATTERNS

¾"
1"
1¼"

~ Yo-yo Pillow ~

Yo-yos, little round puffs of gathered fabric joined into quilts, were made into popular coverlets during the 1930s and 1940s. Originally created as a way to use fabric scraps, yo-yos today represent a renewed interest in fabric crafts. Here, they bring texture and interest to a simple, knife-edge pillow.

MATERIALS

Tightly woven fabric, 44" to 45"-wide: ⅜ yard brown, or desired background color, and ½ yard yellow, or desired color for yo-yos

Sewing thread to match fabrics

Polyester fiberfill for stuffing

TOOLS

Pencil

Compass

Cardboard

Scissors

Sewing needles

Straight pins

Steam iron (optional)

FINISHED SIZE: 12" BY 16"

MAKING THE YO-YOS

For the pillow front and back, cut two 13-by-17-inch rectangles from the backing fabric.

To make a template for the yo-yos, use a compass to draw a circle 4 inches in diameter on the cardboard and cut it out. Use this template and a pencil to mark 35 circles on the wrong side of the yellow fabric. Cut out the fabric circles.

To make each yo-yo, turn under ¼ inch along the outside edge and hand-sew running stitches along this edge (a). Then pull the stitches to gather the circle tightly in the center and knot the thread to secure the gathers (b).

To flatten the circles, press them with a steam iron. Press them with the hole side facing up and with the hole centered.

MAKING THE PILLOW TOP

With the pillow front right side up, arrange the yo-yos with their hole sides facing up in the center of the rectangle in 5 rows of 7 yo-yos. The yo-yos should touch each other at the top and bottom and the center of each side. Pin the yo-yos securely in place, then slipstitch each one around the edges to secure it onto the pillow front.

ASSEMBLING THE PILLOW

To make the pillow, place the front and back pieces together with right sides facing. Stitch around three sides and all four corners, ½ inch from edge, and leave a 5-inch opening on one side. Clip the seam allowances at the corners diagonally, then turn the pillow cover to the right side. Use a pin to pull out the corners. Stuff the cover plumply with fiberfill. Turn the open edges ½ inch to the inside and slipstitch them closed.

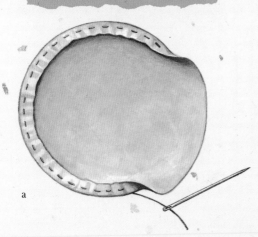

a

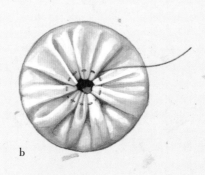

b

Crushed Velvet Patchwork Pillow

The simplest of all patchwork is the one-patch—same-size squares joined in no particular pattern. Elevating this humble design is the use of luxurious fabrics such as velvet, silk, and rayon, and the manipulation of the fabric for a dimensional, exquisitely tactile effect.

MATERIALS

Small amounts of five or more assorted velvet fabrics in the same color palette—here, black, red, and gold

18"-square of velvet for the pillow back

⅜ yard muslin fabric

Sewing thread to match fabrics

16"-square pillow form

2 large tassels (or one window tieback)

TOOLS

Straight pins

Sewing needle

FINISHED SIZE: 16" SQUARE

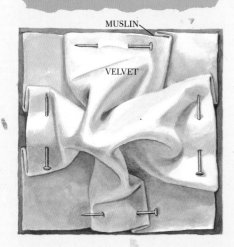

MUSLIN

VELVET

MAKING THE PATCHES

From the muslin, cut 48 3-inch squares, for the foundation. From the velvet fabrics, cut a total of 48 5-inch squares. To make one patch, place a velvet square right side up on top of a muslin square. Pinch, crush, and bunch up the velvet at the center to bring its edges more or less even with the edges of the muslin square. Pin the edges, keeping the pin heads facing out. Turn the piece over, and pulling out the pins as you go, stitch all around the square, ¼ inch from edge of the muslin. Trim the edges of the velvet even with the muslin edges.

ASSEMBLING THE PILLOW TOP

Arrange the patches in 8 rows of 8 squares each, keeping squares of the same fabric separated and evenly distributed. Experiment until you are satisfied with the arrangement.

Working row by row, join the patches together as follows: With right sides facing, pin two squares together and stitch ½ inch from the edge. Press the seam open, then replace the squares in the arrangement.

Place the next square in the row on top of the preceding one, right sides facing, and stitch together ½ inch from the edge; press the seam open. Continue this way, stitching all 8 squares in each row.

Stitch the rows together as follows: Pin first two rows together, right sides facing. To align corners and seams, place the pins at the seams of each row. To reduce bulk, also pin along seam allowances so they stay open and flat. Remove pins as you go. Press the seams open, and press the completed pillow from the wrong side.

ASSEMBLING THE PILLOW

With right sides together, center the pillow top on the backing fabric. Pin generously all around. Stitch around three sides and all four corners, ½ inch from the edge; leave the center 10 inches of one side open. Clip the corners diagonally and turn the pillow cover to the right side. Insert the pillow form. Turn the open edges of the cover ½ inch to the inside, and slipstitch closed. Tack the tassels to one corner.

Whig Rose Table Runner

This table runner is made of five antique, appliquéd blocks no doubt intended to be part of a quilt that was never completed. Unassembled quilt squares are sometimes available at flea markets, but a manageable project such as this one is a perfect opportunity to try appliqué. The freezer-paper method puts a modern spin on tradition, and guarantees crisp, precise results.

MATERIALS

Tightly woven, pre-shrunk cotton, 44" to 45" wide: 2¾ yards white or natural muslin, for background and backing; ¾ yard each red, yellow, and green, for the appliqués

Cardboard

Sewing thread to match fabrics

3 yards white flannel or fusible batting for filler (optional)

TOOLS

Clear quilter's ruler or T square

Dressmaker's marking pencil

Scissors

Pencil

Tracing paper

White paper

Glue

Straight pins

Sewing needles

Steam iron

Freezer paper (optional)

Tweezers (optional)

FINISHED SIZE: 18" BY 90"

CUTTING THE FABRIC

Cut the background squares and the backing from the white fabric. Using a quilter's ruler or T square and a dressmaker's marking pencil, mark and cut out five 19-inch squares for the background and one 19-by-91-inch rectangle for the backing.

MAKING THE TEMPLATES

To complete the quarter patterns A, B, and C (on page 155) for the center blossom, trace each shape onto a piece of paper that has been folded in half vertically then horizontally, with the fold lines aligned with the long dash lines. Cut out each shape. Then trace the actual-size patterns for D, E, F, and one for G. Glue these shapes to cardboard; let the glue dry, then cut out the templates.

Using the templates and a dressmaker's marking pencil, trace the appliqués on the wrong side of the fabric. Keep the shapes ½ inch apart. Trace the largest pieces first, then the smaller ones. Cut out the pieces as indicated below, adding ¼-inch seam allowances all around each shape.

You will need the following number of pieces: From the red fabric, cut 5 A, 5 C, 20 D, and 20 F. From the yellow fabric, cut 5 B and 20 E. From the green fabric, cut 60 G. Also cut 20 bias strips, ⅞ by 6 ½ inches, for the stems or H.

TWO WAYS TO APPLIQUÉ

There are two ways to appliqué by hand. The traditional technique, called needle-turned appliqué, takes a little more time but results in a softer, puffier appliqué. To appliqué this way, hand-sew the shape in place along the seam line, turning under the seam allowances a little at a time with the point of the needle as you stitch (a, page 154), using a slipstitch (b, page 154). Press the finished piece with a pressing cloth to avoid flattening the appliqués too much.

The freezer-paper appliqué method is a technique that ensures crisp edges but

yields flat appliqués; the finished piece must be lined. To use this method, mark and cut a freezer-paper shape without seam allowance for each fabric piece. Center the freezer-paper shape, coated side up, on the wrong side of the fabric shape (c). Fold the seam allowance over the paper edges and use an iron on a medium setting to fuse the fabric in place, creasing the edges of the fabric. Then fuse the appliqué to the background fabric by pressing it in place. Slipstitch the appliqué in place. Cut small slits in the background fabric behind the appliqué and use tweezers to peel away the freezer paper and pull it out through the slit (d).

APPLIQUÉING EACH BLOCK

After you have chosen the method you want to use for appliquéing, make each block sep-arately. To make one block, first make a complete blossom by appliquéing the small blossom pieces to the medium pieces, then appliquéing the medium pieces to the large pieces. For the stems, turn the long edges ¼ inch to the wrong side. Fold each white backing square diagonally in half in both directions and press. Unfold the square. Pin and baste the appliqués in place on the block. Center the large blossom. Curve stems gracefully, roughly following the diagonal creases on the background fabric, and pin them in place. Arrange three leaves in a slightly different way along each stem. Insert the ends of the leaves under the stems and the ends of the stems under the blossoms. To stitch the stems, slipstitch along the inside (concave line) of a curve before stitching the outside (convex line) of the curve.

ASSEMBLING THE RUNNER

Join the five completed blocks in a row with ½ inch seam allowances. Press the seams to one side. For an optional filler, cut flannel to the same size as the backing fabric, 19" by 91", and baste it to the wrong side of the backing fabric. Or, cut fusible batting ½ inch smaller all around, center it on the wrong side of the backing and fuse it in place, following the manufacturer's instructions.

Place the runner top and backing together, with right sides facing, and stitch around three sides and all four corners, ½ inch from the edge, leaving a 6-inch opening on one end. Trim the seam allowance at the corners diagonally and turn the runner right side out. Use a pin to pull out the corners, then fold in the open edges and slipstitch them closed.

NEEDLE-TURNED APPLIQUÉ METHOD

FREEZER-PAPER APPLIQUÉ METHOD

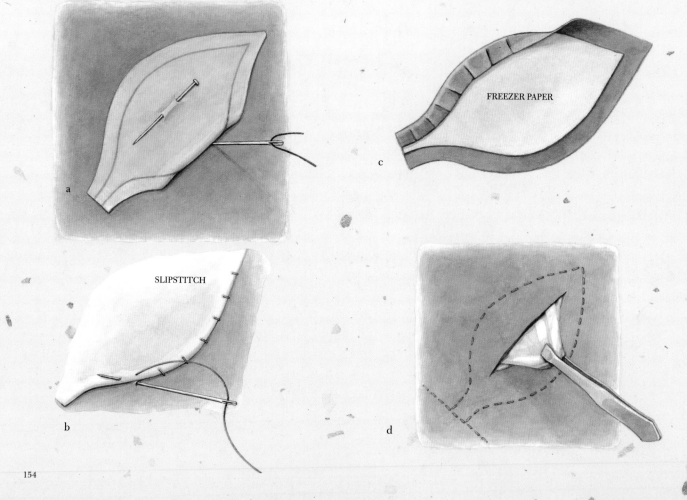

FREEZER PAPER

SLIPSTITCH

a

b

c

d

154

Patterns for the Appliqués

ACTUAL-SIZE PATTERNS

A Quilt Scrap Bunny

An old tattered quilt becomes an adorable stuffed animal by using parts of the quilt that are not torn or threadbare. Use prints and colors in the quilt to best advantage so the muzzle stands out.

MATERIALS

Quilt fragment or pre-quilted fabric

Sewing thread to match fabric

Polyester fiberfill for stuffing

TOOLS

Pencil

Tracing paper

Scissors

Pins

Sewing needle

FINISHED SIZE: 15" TALL

CUTTING OUT THE PIECES

Trace the actual-size patterns on pages 158–159 onto tracing paper, or photocopy them, making two copies of the arm and leg patterns. Cut out the patterns, which include ¼ inch seam allowances.

Fold the quilted fabric in half along a patchwork seam. Place the body pattern (a half pattern) so the long dash lines lie along the fold. Place the arm and leg patterns on the fabric, reversing the second pattern of each. Arrange the other pattern pieces, using the patchwork design to best advantage. Pin in place and cut out as follows: one head back, two each head side, muzzle, and body pieces (one each for the front and back), and four each ear, arm, and leg pieces.

SEWING AND ASSEMBLY

Following the directions below, pin the pieces together with right sides facing, matching the edges to be joined. Sew ¼ inch from the edge. Clip into the seam allowances along curves and at angles. Turn the pieces right side out through the openings. Use the eraser end of a pencil to push ears and legs through, and to push stuffing into hard-to-reach areas. Stuff all but the ear pieces firmly with fiberfill. Turn in all open edges ¼ inch and slip-stitch closed.

MAKING THE HEAD

Pin the head side pieces together and stitch from A to B and from C to D. Pin the muzzle pieces together and stitch from B to C around the deeper curve. Pin the joined muzzle to the open area in the head, matching B and C points. Stitch all around; this completes the head front. Pin the ears together in pairs and stitch around all but short, straight end. Turn, but do not stuff. Pin the ears to the head front with raw edges even, and matching E points. Pin the head front to the head back, matching all the points, and stitch all around, leaving the bottom edge open. Stuff the head.

MAKING THE BODY

Pin an arm piece to each armhole on both body pieces, matching G and H points. Place the body front and back pieces right sides together, matching arms and edges. Stitch the shoulders from F to G, around the arm to H, and then down to I on both sides. Turn right side out. Fold under the bottom edge ¼ inch and pin in place for now.

Pin the legs together in matching pairs. Stitch around them, leaving the straight top edges open. Stuff the legs to within 1 inch of the openings. Insert tops of the legs into bottom of the body, with the leg seams at the center and with all J points matching. Either machine top-stitch across the bottom of the body or slipstitch this seam. Stuff body and arms. Insert head into top opening, matching F points. With a double strand of thread, slipstitch the head securely to the body.

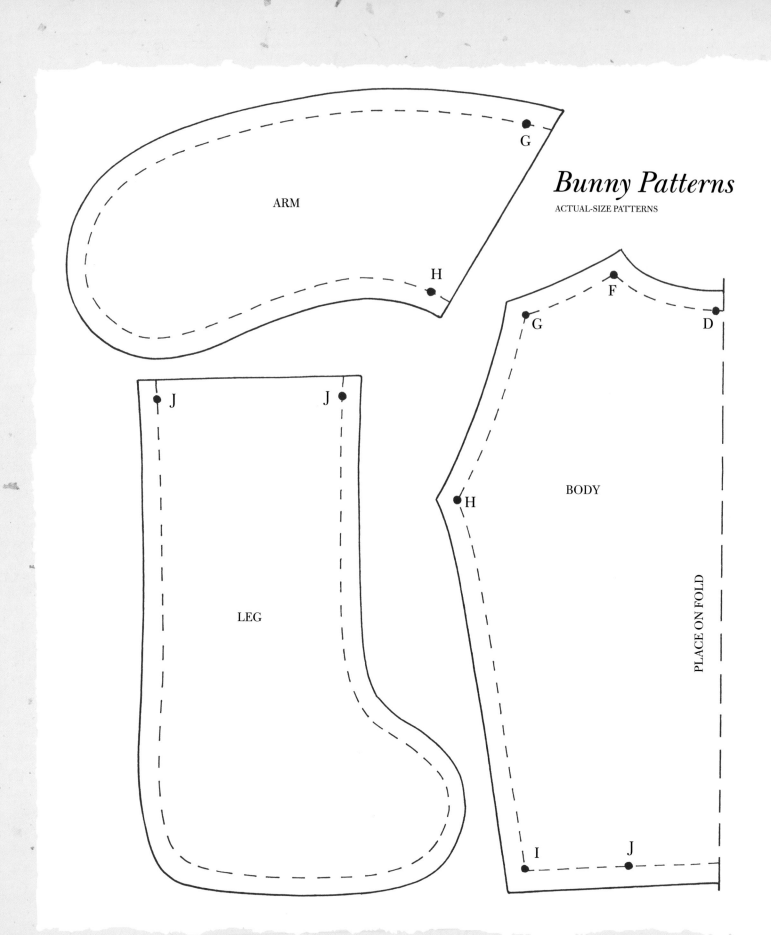

ARM

Bunny Patterns

ACTUAL-SIZE PATTERNS

G

H

F

G

D

BODY

H

LEG

J

J

PLACE ON FOLD

I

J

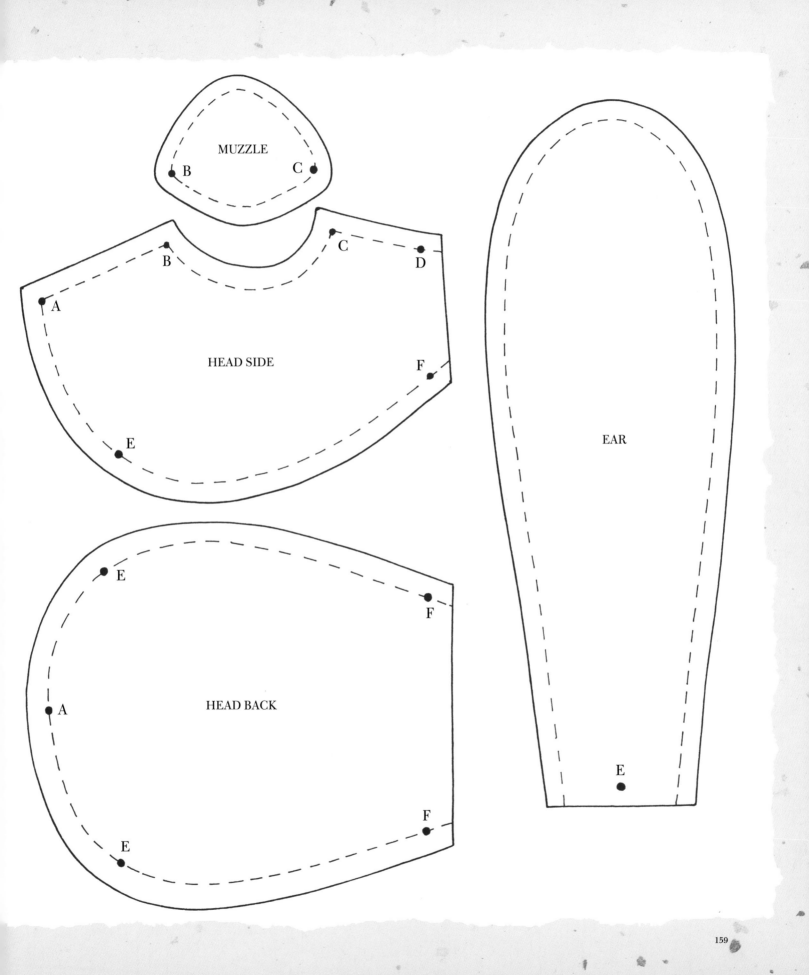

MUZZLE

HEAD SIDE

HEAD BACK

EAR

a link with the
PAST

hink of your favorite house. It may be your own house, the home of a friend, or a place you've visited on vacation. Now ask yourself how the house was furnished. More than likely, there were a few old things that caught your eye and had a tale to tell. Houses steal our hearts when they're personal, warm, and welcoming. And, for many of us, what makes them that way are the timeworn objects that are on display. One country enthusiast, who describes her surroundings as "early attic," says the hand-me-

Everything made a journey from farm to foyer (opposite): the carpenter's sawhorse table, a nineteenth-century weather vane, the weathered boards recycled as a mirror frame, even the wooden bucket that now spouts fresh flowers. Bits of broken china are reincarnated as a bumpy plate (right) that pieces together many memories.

downs that fill her house connect her to the past. For a coffee table, she uses her grandfather's trunk, brought over from Sweden. Her children's silver baby cups are on display in the bathroom, filled with cotton balls. She sleeps under her mother's white Marseilles bedspread every night. She's surrounded by family! Living with old things strengthens our bond to days of long ago.

If you doubt the pull of the past, consider the popularity of country inns, where old furniture, a warm fireplace, fresh flowers, home-cooked food, and a leisurely ambience speak to a way of life that's all but gone. People are re-creating this past by bringing it into their lives, at home, in the workplace, in home offices, and in the marketplace. The most interesting pieces in our homes are often the old things, and when we think about passing something to the next generation, it is usually something that has history and a story behind it.

Some of us are born with a fondness for old things, and some of us develop it as we grow. The thrill of the hunt is irresistible. We haunt antiques shops, brake for garage sales, and drive vans and pickup trucks to haul things home. Devotees are everywhere. For every relic discarded on the street by an indifferent owner, there are two people fighting curbside over who's going to take it home. Even when that relic is of questionable value, there's always someone who will covet it. "One man's trash is another man's treasure" is the truth that makes garage sales lively and keeps them going year after year.

If you're an inveterate junker, you're used to hearing (and ignoring) remarks such as "What does she see in that old thing?" If you have a knack for seeing the possibilities in objects, it opens up a world of opportunity. Take the split skin off an old drum and it's a magazine holder. A copper washtub holds logs by the fireplace. An old hatbox filled with letters, photographs, or potpourri becomes a

An eccentric accent piece often puts a whole new spin on a room. In the renovated cottage (opposite), a fanciful Victorian mantelpiece reprises its original role in new surroundings, adding a note of softness to a rugged fireplace trimmed with native river rocks. Fat floral cushions spruce up the collection of rustic, weathered chairs.

Turn convention inside out by using outdoor architectural details indoors. A Chippendale pediment probably crafted for the top of a front door stands in for a headboard (above). Its grouping of tiny framed pictures spills to a lower shelf sheathed with a lettuce-edged dresser scarf. In a remodeled bathroom (opposite), a marble shelf rests on a pair of architectural elements that once decorated the outside of a house. Linens are stowed in the steamer trunk, and towels hang on a nineteenth-century coat tree. Leaded bull's-eye windows from the 1800s, original to the house, provide privacy for the room yet let in the light.

treasured keepsake. It's worthwhile to keep an eye out for treasures that can be cherished as is, or transformed into something else. These treasures fall into two categories: respectable and bohemian. Both types are worth looking for. Respectable old things are waxed and polished, and stand with perfect posture. They can be found in antiques stores. Bohemians are found with their feet in the grass, or slouching on the stones, in someone's driveway. They can be bartered, traded for, or had for almost nothing at yard sales, garage sales, and church rummage sales. Spruced up with paint, polish, or a cleaning rag, they often end up rivaling their well-bred cousins in looks and personality.

There are some rules for finding these treasures: Get out among the stuff. Consider using things in new ways. Turn nothing much into something special,

either on your own or with the help of an expert refinisher, upholsterer, or painter. Develop a relationship with several antiques dealers. Ask them to alert you when something unusual comes in. Visit a consortium of dealers or an antiques cooperative regularly. Go to shows, and get on mailing lists for estate sales and auctions. Attend annual antiques extravaganzas. Note the dates of town trash days and go out searching for dynamic discards the night before, with flashlight in hand and a big station wagon to cart off your finds.

Next, find a mentor—someone whose taste you admire and who is willing to share his or her expertise. Shop with that person. Ask why that person buys things, and practice seeing things in fresh new ways. Sometimes mimicking is the best way to learn. Get inside someone's head. The easiest way to develop a

Retired doesn't have to mean obsolete. An antique water filter topped with a marble slice becomes the base for a cozy cafe table in the corner of a sunny kitchen (opposite). The sideboard in the second-floor great room of a Colonial-style farmhouse in Ohio (above) is an 1820 dry sink with original paint. The wooden bowl on the table is as useful holding apples as cradling rising dough, as it did years ago. Retired to the wall, a well-loved pachisi game board is savored today for its graphic look and timeworn colors.

creative eye is to spend time with creative people and see how they operate.

Turning something into something else is sleight of hand, magic, recycling at its best. Instead of thinking that old piece of junk would be better off on a bonfire, develop a critical eye and an inquisitive air. Ask yourself what you could do with it. Ask yourself "What if" and the options abound.

At an estate sale, while everyone else is looking through the house, the curious treasure hunter is out in the barn, envisioning sawhorses as desk legs, a wooden crate as a display shelf. The treasure hunter sees a worn wood bucket as an eccentric planter that can take the geraniums through summer with charm, for the same price as a plastic pot. A tired quilt? Instead of dumping it, the treasure hunter makes a window valance, hiding rips in the folds of the fabric.

New ideas also percolate far from home. Travel outside your usual circles. Visit historic houses and museum room settings. Take a house tour, or visit artists' lofts, which are sometimes opened to the public as a fund-raising effort for an art school or museum. Artists see things differently than most of us and can offer a lesson on how to improvise with a free spirit.

Make a practice of stopping in interesting shops when you go away for the weekend. Even a business trip sometimes affords a few free hours. Shopkeepers show a unique vision through their wares, and you may stumble across a piece you've never seen before, or see something displayed in a new way that sparks a fresh idea; maybe you have something similar at home. It's an herb-drying rack, but why not hang pots from it? It's a coat stand, but it could be the perfect place to show off vintage linens. You may not know how you're going to use something, but if it speaks to you, buy it. Fabric discovered on an anniversary trip to Italy may turn out to be just right for reupholstering dining chairs the

Reinvention can be an inspired way to use something old in a new setting. The painted window shutters (opposite) had no traditional purpose for the owner of this Florida home, but their color was so nice they were impossible to toss out. Mounting them side by side on the wall of the kitchen rejuvenated them and provided a way to show off a collection of woodenware and graniteware, each piece artfully hooked to the wooden slats.

following year. An ornate frame, bought for a song and sitting in the shed, is eventually refinished and becomes a mirror.

Relatives can provide your link with the past: a great aunt's beautifully embroidered handkerchiefs, a cousin's seashell collection, Grandfather's polished mahogany rocker. But not everyone has relatives with treasures to leave behind; in that case, adopt some. Antiques shops are filled with handiwork from generations of anonymous artisans. Their creations can substitute for the heirlooms you might have inherited from a grandmother or parent. Take home a stenciled cupboard, a quirky corner shelf made of wooden spools, a rocking chair of twigs, a dollhouse made with love, or a portrait of someone you've never met. These things, completed so long ago, can bring anyone a piece of the past.

In a room with little storage (opposite), the corner cupboard is a make-do, put together from two separate pieces: a columned door frame and a pair of cupboard doors that show off beautiful grain-painting, although the scraping was abandoned midproject. In the dining room of a turn-of-the-century farmhouse in Vermont (above), a meticulously restored 1860s dried-bean cupboard once used in a country store now serves as a whimsical sideboard. Everyday silverware is kept in the round storage boxes made of tin and wood.

Things that have long outgrown their original use can be helpful in different ways. Deemed past its prime for fancy or sedate surroundings, the painted three-drawer dresser (above) suits this casual sunporch to a T; it has become a potting table massed with flowers. On the sun-streaked porch (opposite), violets and vinca thrive in a hanging shelf made from a wooden bakery box with handholds visible on the sides. The box came from Helms Bakery, which used to sell baked goods door-to-door in southern California. The child's chalkboard conveys messages.

Shelves for displaying favorite flea market finds and cherished keepsakes can be created from objects with unusual and unexpected origins. Handmade shoes and boots dried on this wooden shoemaker's rack long ago (opposite); now colorful pottery, quilts, and Fioriware pitchers and platters are showcased on the foot-shaped slats. Recycling was part of everyday life back in the 1870s, when this imaginative corner shelf (above left) was fashioned from wooden thread spools. A tobacco sorter (above right) once graded the long brown leaves by size; now, set on its side, it is the perfect place to exhibit small figurines, including German sheep that were part of village scenes often displayed under Christmas trees.

Salvaged from a Spanish church, a delicate ironwork screen is the lacy backdrop for a double bed (above). The screen soars toward the gables of this attic room and emphasizes its height. Lost-and-found is an exciting pastime in the Maryland house (opposite) where a rusty cemetery fence topped with a stone slab serves as a sleek hall table; the columns on either side of the table were salvaged from an old Southern mansion. Outside on the patio, spiral columns from another old house are used as plant stands.

Coffee tables come in all guises. The wooden sleigh provides a striking note in the rustic living room (opposite), and still looks rugged enough to take a run down the hills that surround this Colorado log home. A sculptor's iron trolley (above left) makes an ingenious table with a shiny outsize surface that is impervious to spills. Easily rolled from place to place, its industrial design is a sturdy counterpoint to softer surroundings. A wooden lobster trap topped with glass (above right) makes a charming table in front of the fire. The 1820s pine mantel, about 100 years older than the house, served another fireplace in good stead for years before being transplanted here.

When the decor is imaginative, why settle for a traditional coffee table? In a glassed-in living room overlooking a ravine (opposite), the view is woodsy, and so are the furnishings, including a 1780 footed grain bin that serves as a coffee table; the storage inside is a plus. At a shore house with limited space (top left), a little bench is more practical than a full-size coffee table, performing at times as a book rest, a movable footstool, or a place to set a drink. A white bench with a fanciful carved apron provides extra seating against the wall, and an old-time vegetable-store bin serves as a sofa table. A blue workbench (bottom left) is just the right height for a tea party, anchoring a ring of fanciful twig chairs.

Certain fabrics can evoke an era with just a glance; that's how it is with chenille. The cushions of the generous wicker sofa (above) have been covered with remnants of vintage chenille bedspreads, bringing back the 1950s in a rush. Pillows made from pieces of needlework collected by the homeowner add to the sofa's charm. You can put timeless quilts to work in a brand-new way that's energy-saving besides. Three different quilts suspended from wooden rings create a one-of-a-kind window treatment for a cheerful living room (opposite). The quilts, all different in design, have a similar color scheme that echoes the room's softly colored and timeworn 1930s furnishings.

Photo Credits

1 Keith Scott Morton
2 Lilo Raymond
4-5 Doug Kennedy
6-7 Paul Kopelow
8 Keith Scott Morton
9 Paul Kopelow
10-11 Paul Kopelow
12 Kari Haavisto
13 Keith Scott Morton
14 Paul Kopelow
15 Doug Kennedy
17 William Stites
18-19 Keith Scott Morton
20 left Doug Kennedy
20 right Allan Baille
    and Debra De Boise
21 Feliciano
22 Paul Kopelow
23-27 Keith Scott Morton
28 Jessie Walker
29 John Vaughn
30-31 Keith Scott Morton
32-33 Keith Scott Morton
35 top Keith Scott Morton
35 bottom Jeremy Samuelson
37 Keith Scott Morton
39 Paul Kopelow
41 Keith Scott Morton
43 Keith Scott Morton
45 Jessie Walker
46 Doug Kennedy
49-59 Keith Scott Morton
60 Jessie Walker
61 Paul Kopelow
62 Doug Kennedy

63 top Keith Scott Morton
63 bottom Keith Scott Morton
65 Keith Scott Morton
67-68 Jessie Walker
71-77 Keith Scott Morton
78 Jessie Walker
79-80 Keith Scott Morton
82 Peter Vitale
83 Keith Scott Morton
84 Jessie Walker
85 Keith Scott Morton
86 Paul Kopelow
87 Al Teufen
89-91 Jessie Walker
92-101 Keith Scott Morton
103 Paul Kopelow
107 Keith Scott Morton
111 Feliciano
115 Keith Scott Morton
116 Peter Margonelli
117-118 Jessie Walker
120-121 Keith Scott Morton
122 John Vaughn
123 Jessie Walker
124 top Keith Scott Morton
124 bottom Philip Thompson
125-127 Keith Scott Morton
128-129 Peter Vitale
130 Keith Scott Morton
131 left Keith Scott Morton
131 right Jessie Walker
132-134 Keith Scott Morton
135 Jessie Walker
136 Paul Kopelow
137-139 Keith Scott Morton

141 Al Teufen
145 Jessie Walker
149 Keith Scott Morton
151 Keith Scott Morton
153 Ralph Bogertman
157 Paul Kopelow
160 John Vaughn
161 Keith Scott Morton
162 Jeremy Samuelson
164 Jessie Walker
165 Paul Kopelow
166 Pizzi/Thompson
167 Al Teufen
169 Paul Kopelow
170 Keith Scott Morton
171 Paul Kopelow
172 Keith Scott Morton
173 Jeremy Samuelson
174 Jessie Walker
175 left Keith Scott Morton
175 right Jessie Walker
176 Feliciano
177 Keith Scott Morton
178 Jessie Walker
179 left Keith Scott Morton
179 right Keith Scott Morton
180 Jessie Walker
181 top Keith Scott Morton
181 bottom Jessie Walker
182 Jessie Walker
183 Keith Scott Morton
184 Keith Scott Morton
186 Keith Scott Morton
192 Keith Scott Morton

Index

Page numbers in italics refer to illustrations.

Country Living would like to thank

the many homeowners, designers, and architects

whose work appears on these pages.